SIX DROWN SAVING CHICKEN

P9-CJR-212

SIX DROWN SAVING CHICKEN

and other true stories from the Reuters "Oddly Enough" file

by Reuters

Carroll & Graf Publishers, Inc.
New York

Copyright © 1996 by Reuters

All rights reserved

First edition 1996

Carroll & Graf Publishers, Inc.
260 Fifth Avenue
New York, NY 10001

ISBN 0-7867-0369-5

Library of Congress Cataloging-in-Publication Data is available.

Manufactured in the United States of America.

Contents

Introduction by Robert Basler, News Editor, Reuters America

Over the past century and a half, Reuters has built up the world's most comprehensive and complete news-gathering machine. Our foreign correspondents, cameramen and photographers collect information in the farthest-flung places one could name, and serve it up in the form of text, television, pictures and graphics—from Kiev to Karachi, Beirut to Beijing, Denver to Dublin. Our news is seen and heard on trading room financial screens, in newspapers, on television and radio, and on the Internet.

And, when you cast your net that far and wide for that much serious news, you're bound to pick up some strange things as well.

The guy in London who got free drinks in a pub by making up a story about having a terminal illness, and did it so well that a sympathetic listener put him out of his misery. The "wurst" burglar in Copenhagen, who fell into a vat of sausage dye. The exploding Romanian pig. The fainting Indian hangman. The topless Australian barber shop. The San Francisco toe-licker . . .

Clearly, there is a reason why these stories are called human interest. There is a tremendous fascination with them. With our network of more than 125 bureaus around the world, we are equally at home recording the quirky crime in Texas, the poignant pet story in London or the cannibal ritual in Irian Jaya. Strange crimes, quirks of human nature, the grotesque, the tragic, the absurd.

Reuters has been issuing these odd stories among the weightier news for years, just to give people something to shake their heads at when the big headlines get a little overwhelming. Some of these items are remarkable because they illustrate events that are routine in one culture but far from it in another. Some of them, on the other hand, would be bizarre anyplace.

A few years ago Reuters began sprinkling some of these stories into our network of financial screen information, right there between the economic indicators and the municipal bond analyses, and somewhat to our surprise our odd features were an overnight success among traders. Within weeks, these stories were consistently on our top-ten-most-read list.

Thinking back on it, Reuters shouldn't have been at all surprised by this. People are people, and they have an endless capacity for amazing one another, even in the midst of billion-dollar foreign exchange deals.

This year, building on the popularity of these items among our newspaper, broadcast and financial customers, Reuters began offering them online as well, in the form of a product called "Oddly Enough." At a number of Web sites, Internet users can find our curious nuggets.

In newspaper jargon, these pieces are commonly called *brights*, although obviously many of them are anything but funny. Sometimes, the more accurate—if oxymoronic—name of *gothic brights* is applied to them. They are the yarns we talk about at work and at play, the stories we often clip and save.

Not all correspondents are able to recognize those items which may seem mundane in their part of the world but which would seem amazing someplace else, so this book owes a real debt to those with that special radar. The appetite for these stories is pretty close to universal, and while Americans are enthusiastic consumers of gothic brights, they are generous producers of them as well; to much of the world, U.S. culture is perplexing and confusing, and home-grown American brights are gobbled up overseas.

Because Reuters has dealt with paper and ink for so many, many years, it seemed appropriate to take some of the better pieces and publish them in book form so people can read them, hold onto them and pass them around. We hope you agree.

Crime

ROBBERS TEAM UP WITH RATS

DUBLIN - Forget guns. Irish robbers have found rats are a more effective weapon to frighten people into abandoning cars and possessions, police said.

Dublin police said robbers toss rodents into an open window or sun roof and wait for their terrified victims—usually women—to flee.

"The ladies approach traffic lights and when stopped they come and throw the rats in," a police spokesman said. "Usually the lady jumps out and they then steal the car or take the victim's possessions at leisure."

The spokesman said they were advising victims to take their chances with the rats.

NOISY THIEVES WAKE VILLAGE

LONDON - Thieves woke a sleepy British village in the early hours of the morning as they dragged a safe behind their car.

Police inspector Andy Shearing said the thieves tied a rope round the safe after breaking into a post office in the village of Maiden Bradley in southwest England.

"Obviously it made a great deal of noise as it clattered down the village high street behind the car," Shearing said.

Police are questioning one man about the raid and would like to talk to at least two more.

MAN RUN OVER BY OWN CAR AFTER REPORTING IT STOLEN

LONDON - A Briton was run over by his own car moments after leaving a police station where he had reported it stolen.

Richard Weston from Nottingham, central England, stepped out of the police station and saw his car waiting at traffic lights.

He ran in front of the vehicle to stop it but the thieves accelerated, hitting the 23-year-old and hurling him into the air.

Weston was treated in hospital for internal injuries. The car thieves got away.

WRONG LIGHT AT THE END OF THE TUNNEL

NEW DELHI, India - A group of burglars dug a tunnel to rob a jeweler's shop in New Delhi but ended up in a washing machine store next door, the Indian Express newspaper reported.

The burglars apparently found the washing machines too big to carry, and had to make do with a collection of religious statuettes kept in the shop, the newspaper said.

A 15-foot tunnel was found linked to the sewer system, a shop assistant said.

The shopowner found a strong stench and discovered a hole on his floor, which revealed the tunnel. Several small tunnels had been dug to find a way to the shop, Indian Express said.

MATH PROBLEMS FEATURE DRUGS, VIOLENCE

CHICAGO - An inner-city elementary school teacher was suspended after he gave his class math problems involving drug dealing, prostitution and car theft.

Among the test questions was one involving a pimp named Rufus who needed to know how many $65 "tricks" his three "girls" would have to perform to support his $800-per-day crack habit, the Chicago Sun-Times reported.

The teacher was relieved of his duties at his school while an investigation was underway, the newspaper said.

Other questions on the examination given to the 11- to 13-year-old children last week involved a drug dealer figuring out how much to dilute his heroin to maximize his profit and an auto thief deciding what models of cars to steal.

HOLY MOLAR! WHAT A CRIME

JOHANNESBURG, South Africa - A worker woke up without his false teeth after a robber forced open his mouth in his sleep and escaped with his most prized possession, police said.

Maphupu Molatudi, a 55-year-old "piece job" laborer who has no steady employment but finds work where he can, was beaten up by the robber during the attack which took place at a male migrant workers' hostel north of Johannesburg.

"Mr. Molatudi was asleep in his bed at the Sethokga Hostel in Tembisa when he was attacked. The suspect beat him with fists, grabbed him by the throat and took his false teeth out of his mouth," police spokeswoman Petro Rossouw said.

"The suspect was arrested but the false teeth are still missing. We think he must have destroyed them or thrown them away thinking that then there could be no evidence," she said.

The man is to be charged with robbery.

BREAST SURGERY FRAUD LANDS WOMAN IN JAIL

HONG KONG - An accountant was sentenced to two years in jail for stealing HK$2.6 million (US$338,000) from her Hong Kong employers in order to enlarge her breasts, adjust her eyelids and reshape her eyebrows.

The court heard that the 24-year-old woman stole the cash from the company and used some of it for intensive cosmetic surgery, the South China Morning Post newspaper said.

She pleaded guilty to theft.

BLONDES HAVE LESS FUN IN APELDOORN

AMSTERDAM - Blondes in the Dutch city of Apeldoorn are being victimized by a gang of teenage girls jealous of their good looks, a Dutch newspaper said.

According to De Telegraaf, up to 20 girls aged between 14

and 19 were thought to be responsible for beating up other women—all of them fair-haired.

Police have arrested four and said the girls had confessed that they had been moved by envy to mount a campaign of terror against the city's blondes.

"Up until now 10 victims have come forward, but there are probably many more who won't report the incident for fear of reprisals," the paper quoted the police as saying.

KILLER INSPIRED BY DYLAN ALLOWED TO SEE CONCERT

HOBART, Australia - A man who trampled his mother to death to the accompaniment of Bob Dylan's "One More Cup of Coffee for the Road" was let out of prison for a night to see his idol in concert, Australian Associated Press (AAP) reported.

The 25-year-old man went to Dylan's April 11 concert in Hobart with a guard and nurse from Hobart's Risdon jail, Corrective Services Department official Ben Marris said.

The man killed his 59-year-old mother five years ago at their home after she complained about his playing Dylan's album "Desire" at 4 a.m.

He told police he thought his mother was the evil character Isis on the album and the music had given him strength to kill her. After killing her, he sprinkled instant coffee on the body while a neighbor tried to pull him away.

He was found not guilty of murder on grounds of insanity.

The outing had the blessing of the state attorney general of Tasmania, Ron Cornish, and the medical team treating Dickinson's schizophrenia, Marris told AAP.

He said the concert was the idea of a psychiatric team who said the man had been responding well to treatment.

The medical team had discussed the possibility that Dylan might sing "One More Cup of Coffee for the Road" in the concert but it was decided there was little risk if he did, Marris said.

EX-SCHOOL HEAD GETS SIX YEARS FOR DEATHS

TOKYO - A Japanese court sentenced a former private-school principal to six years in prison for causing the deaths of two students he locked in a sweltering freight-car as a punishment for smoking.

In July, 1991, the man, then principal of Kazenoko Gakuen School for problem children in Hiroshima, handcuffed and confined two students in a windowless freightcar as punishment for smoking cigarettes.

The two, a 14-year-old boy and a 16-year-old girl, died of dehydration after receiving almost no liquids during their 45-hour confinement in intense summer heat.

In his ruling at the Hiroshima District Court, Presiding Judge Kenji Fujito said: "We can't say what the accused did was justifiable educational measures. It was an illegal act."

"What the accused did was far beyond understanding by common sense," Fujito added.

The school, which followed a military-style regimen, attempted to rehabilitate students who refused to attend regular school, through farming and sailing sessions.

The deaths sparked public controversy over draconian school rules and methods of discipline in Japan. In 1983, four students died after being punished at the Spartan Totsuka Yacht School, which also taught problem children.

WOMAN ARRESTED AFTER FROZEN BABY FOUND

LISBON, Portugal - Portuguese police have arrested a 46-year-old woman who kept a dead baby in her refrigerator for nine years, newspapers reported.

The remains were discovered after a power failure last September forced the woman to ask neighbors if she could keep items in their freezer. When she did not reclaim the package, the neighbors opened it and found the body, the papers said.

Prison officials at Tires women's jail outside Lisbon confirmed that the woman was being held there.

According to the press reports, the woman told police that the baby died two weeks after being born prematurely.

When asked why she had frozen the baby, the woman "merely shrugged her shoulders," Lisbon daily O Publico quoted one police official as saying.

MAN CUTS OFF FRIEND'S HEAD IN DRINKING SPREE

WARSAW, Poland - A man cut off his friend's head with an ax while playing a game of dare after a drinking spree, a legal official said.

Andrzej Pazdziorko, a prosecutor in the northwestern Polish town of Stargard, said by telephone the incident occurred after four friends got drunk.

First, 41-year-old Franciszek Z. put his hand on a wooden block and told his friends he was ready to have it cut off to prove how tough he was. None of them reacted.

But when 30-year-old Krzysztof A. put his head on the block in a similar challenge, Franciszek Z. chopped it off. The body was then buried but Z. was later arrested.

"It was a kind of contest," Pazdziorko said, confirming media reports of the killing. He gave no other details.

KILLER GETS THIRD REPRIEVE FROM HANGMAN

NEW DELHI, India - A convicted murderer was granted a third reprieve from the hangman just hours before he was due at the gallows, Indian news agencies said.

Rajgopal Nayyar won the first reprieve when the hangman fainted before carrying out his first execution. The second was ordered by a court in the northern city of Jammu, where he has been jailed for 10 years.

Nayyar, convicted of killing his stepfather and brother over a land dispute, had been due to hang on Friday morning. But the agencies said the Supreme Court met in extraordinary session and gave him another reprieve.

They said it heard a petition by Sikh politician Simranjit Singh Mann asking for the death sentence to be commuted because Nayyar had already spent a long time on death row. It was not clear how Mann became involved.

FAKE PRIEST ARRESTED AFTER 12 YEARS OF GIVING MASS

BOGOTA, Colombia - Colombian police have arrested a man who for 12 years gave mass, baptized babies and married couples as a priest but was actually a fake, the television news program *TV Hoy* reported.

After a local bishop complained, police arrested the man as he was giving mass in a church near Mariquita, over 62 miles northwest of Bogotá, the program said.

It said the bishop denounced the man to police when he learned of the unusual ways he was giving mass and asking people for donations.

But the suspect, who was never ordained as a priest, remained unrepentant. "I'm with God," he told a reporter, "If Jesus went to jail for spreading the Gospel, then I will too."

The program said he had worked in nearly all of the country's provinces throughout his fraudulent years as a priest and had married more than one hundred couples.

The local bishop called on all those who were married by the fake priest to take their vows again before a proper priest.

FAKE FRIAR FOUND OUT

NAPLES, Italy - An Italian swindler, who gave police the slip by living in monasteries and posing as a monk for nearly a year and a half, was arrested after the real friars became suspicious and reported him.

Police said the man had qualified as a novice during his time "inside" but lived a far flashier lifestyle with a hi-fi and color television rigged up in his monk's cell.

He duped monks into trusting him with their valuables and police said they found a safe in his cell containing gold objects, expensive watches, credit cards and bank transactions.

The suspect, a Sicilian with fake papers in the name of Costantino, was arrested in 1992 for a scam in which he posed as an aristocrat.

He was made to report to police under a special surveillance program but fled and took refuge in a monastery near Naples.

MAN BEGS FOR JAIL TO ESCAPE NAGGING MOTHER

ROME - An Italian confined to house arrest has begged police to take him to jail so he can escape his nagging mother, newspapers reported.

They said the 32-year-old was so fed up with his mother's moaning that he telephoned police to see if a cell was free.

"Put me in prison . . . I can't take it any more," he was quoted as saying.

Police advised the man to seek advice from a lawyer or apply through the courts, the reports said.

They said the man, who was not named, lived near the northern town of Brescia and had been put under house arrest pending an appeal against a conviction for armed robbery.

WEDDING GUESTS SEE BESTIALITY VIDEO BY MISTAKE

LONDON - A British man was found guilty of having sex with a dog after a video he made of the act was inadvertently shown to speechless wedding guests expecting to see a replay of a marriage ceremony.

The 59-year-old man lent his video recorder to a friend to film the wedding, but forgot to erase from the tape scenes of himself in sex acts with a neighbor's bull terrier named Ronnie.

The man said the 10-minute film shown to the jury had been

an attempt at trick photography and featured only simulated sex acts. He will be sentenced after psychiatric and other reports have been made available.

MOM IN A JAM OVER STRAWBERRY JELLY

LONDON - A four-year-old boy took revenge on his mother when she refused to dish up his favorite strawberry jelly dessert by reporting her to the police, British newspapers said.

The boy, named Richard, called the police on their emergency 999 number and asked them to "come and sort out" his 32-year-old mother who was insisting he eat his first course before having dessert, said the reports in the tabloid press.

"It was the funniest 999 call we've ever had. We made sure Richard had a huge bowl of jelly after his dinner," a police spokesman was quoted as saying.

The boy's parents have since had a lock put on the telephone at their home in Caerphilly, Wales.

DRUG SUSPECT REFUSES TO MOVE BOWELS

WELLINGTON, New Zealand - A suspected drug courier who has defied New Zealand police by refusing to move his bowels for 23 days alleged that police were misusing their powers.

Police suspect that the 35-year-old man swallowed a heroin-filled condom. Waiting for the proof, they detained him under observation—without arresting or charging him—for 21 days, the maximum permitted under New Zealand's anti-drug laws.

On Friday, three and a half hours before he was due to be released, he was formally arrested and charged with possession of heroin for supply. He was remanded in custody until next Friday.

BURNED BY A TOAST

RIO DE JANEIRO, Brazil - Brazilian police are hunting for a thief who invited a busload of passengers to toast his birthday with drinks laced with drugs before robbing them as they slept, a police investigator said.

The thief chatted with many of the 22 passengers on the bus traveling from the northeastern city of Salvador to Rio de Janeiro before buying them all drinks during a rest stop, Kearney Santos said.

The man slipped some drugs into the drinks and within minutes of resuming their journey, the passengers fell into a deep sleep, he said.

'The driver's cabin is separated from the rest of the passengers," Santos said. "He didn't see a thing."

GIRL'S SHOW AND TELL LEADS TO MOTHER'S ARREST

SYDNEY, Australia - A woman was arrested after her 12-year-old daughter took her mother's marijuana to school to show her class, The Sydney Morning Herald reported.

Teachers at the girls' school contacted police who raided the mother's home in the town of Bakers Creek on the northern Queensland coast after the girl "took mummy's marijuana to school for show and tell," the newspaper said.

The 32-year-old mother pleaded guilty on June 16 to unlawful possession of a dangerous drug and unlawful possession of a pipe. She was fined A$475 (US$350).

BUNGLING BURGLARS BLOW UP FIREWORKS FACTORY

LONDON - A British fireworks factory was destroyed when burglars tried to open its door with an oxyacetylene torch and caused the contents to explode.

Police said the torch set the gang's van on fire. The blaze sent sparks into the concrete building, a World War Two gun emplacement, and set alight tons of fireworks.

"The explosion was such that it virtually demolished the structure," said a police spokesman in Kent, southern England.

The robbers have been dubbed the "hole-in-the-ground gang" by police.

POLICE ARREST "VAMPIRE"

MOSCOW - A man who feasted on the blood of a passer-by after he bit through an artery in his neck has been arrested in the town of Tula about 125 miles south of Moscow, Itar-Tass news agency said.

The 20-year-old homeless man, identified only as S., had lured a drunken man into bushes and bitten through his carotid artery, Tass said.

The "vampire" told police he first developed a taste for blood in the army and had carried out several similar acts in other regions of Russia, Tass said.

"Tula police have never had to deal with a vampire in their 77-year history," it added.

CAR THIEF LEAVES NOTE PREGNANT WITH MEANING

LONDON - A well-mannered thief apologized for stealing a woman's car by leaving a note to say he had to take his pregnant wife to hospital.

When he returned the car, police found a note on the seat saying: "I have never done this before but my wife was having our child and I would have hated to have missed the birth."

He promised to send car owner Carol Richards "15 pounds ($23.69) for any inconvenience caused. Yours, a very sorry person."

The London owner is not convinced: "If the 15 pounds does arrive, then I will believe the story."

FANTASY MAN FOUND GUILTY OF RAPE

NASHVILLE, Tennessee - A Nashville businessman was found guilty of two counts of rape by fraud and one of attempted rape by fraud for tricking two women into sex acts by posing as men they knew.

The 45-year-old man was convicted through a seldom-used Tennessee law, a rewrite of a 1979 law set up to protect married women from men claiming to be their husbands.

The two women, who were in their 20s, testified earlier that they were fooled totally by the man's whispered phone calls.

One woman said the man apparently obtained information about her from a published engagement announcement and pretended to be her fiancee, urging her to go to a motel, disrobe, unlock the door and lie on the bed blindfolded. When she glimpsed him through a window and realized he was not her fiancee, she hastily locked the door.

The second witness, an X-ray technician, testified she thought the man was a boyfriend, and let him into her apartment in the dark where he had sex with her. In a taped statement to police, which was played in court, the man admitted having sex with a number of women after phoning them late at night claiming to be their "fantasy man."

In closing arguments, the man's attorney claimed the

women consented, saying, "You can't talk on the phone to someone 20 or 30 minutes and think they are someone else."

MAN ARRESTED FOR 18,000 PRANK PHONE CALLS

TOKYO - Japanese police have arrested a 47-year-old restaurant employee for making around 18,000 prank phone calls to a hospital since February last year, a spokesman said.

The spokesman for northern Tokyo's Itabashi police said the man placed the daily calls from his home and from public telephone booths to an Itabashi public hospital.

Most were silent calls but at times, he played taped military songs, the police said.

The man worked for a firm catering to the hospital but quit after the hospital lodged complaints about his behavior, the spokesman said.

Then, from February 1994, he began making daily calls to the hospital. Hospital workers finally alerted police in August after a year and a half of the harassment, which continued until his arrest.

JUST MAKE THAT CHECK OUT TO KIDNAPPERS, INC.

MANILA, The Philippines - Kidnapping has become such a way of life in the Philippines that gangs now accept checks to cover their ransom demands, an anti-crime watch group said.

At least three Filipino-Chinese businessmen were quickly freed by their kidnappers recently after they issued checks ranging from 300,000 pesos to one million pesos ($11,500 to $38,460), the Movement for Restoration of Peace and Order said.

"I doubt if they gave stop-payment instructions because the kidnappers would certainly have gotten back to them," said one of the officials, who asked not to be named.

"CINDERELLA" CLEARED OF THEFT

RIMINI, Italy - A woman was cleared of theft in a case of "Cinderella" in reverse when the judge made her try on a shoe left at the scene of the crime and it did not fit.

Claudia Zanella walked away free from a court in the Adriatic resort of Rimini. Her size 37 foot was lost in the size 39 shoe, Italian newspapers reported.

Zanella, 48, had been accused of shoplifting and assault. Part of the evidence was a high-heeled shoe lost by the fleeing shoplifter.

MAN ARRESTED FOR TRYING TO SELL BABY IN STREET

NEW YORK - A 37-year-old man was charged with trying to sell his four-month-old son in the streets of New York for $1,000, authorities said, but under current law his actions only rank as a misdemeanor.

Authorities said the man walked around the streets of Queens, offering to sell the baby to passers-by for $1,000 at least three separate times.

He is charged with endangering the welfare of a child, attempted abandonment and violating the state's social services law, which prohibits the sale of a child.

He faces up to a year in prison on each count.

The baby is back with its mother, who told a local television station that the whole incident was a misunderstanding on the part of authorities.

FIREMAN BURNED FOR RECOGNITION

GRENOBLE, France - An arsonist fireman who helped put out his own fires out of a burning desire for public esteem was sent to prison for 18 months in the French spa town of Thonon-les-Bains, court officials said.

The 25-year-old volunteer fireman admitted in court to having set fire to several buildings and cars in the Alpine resort on the south shore of Lake Geneva last year.

He then alerted firemen and helped them control the blazes in order to earn "recognition and esteem."

HOMEMADE CASH MACHINE FRAUDSTERS JAILED

LONDON - Three Britons were jailed for swindling bank customers of $186,000 using the world's first homemade bank cash-dispensing machine.

When people tried without success to get cash from the machine, the trio secretly recorded their bank details and personal identity numbers (PINs) and used the information to siphon money from the customers' accounts with real banks.

More than 300 people were fooled by the machine, which was set in the wall of what appeared to be a mortgage broker's office in east London and boasted signs showing it could be used by customers holding certain plastic cash cards.

At the men's trial earlier this month, Southwark Crown Court in south London heard the gang's plot was the first of its type in the world known to have succeeded.

A U.S. gang last year used a stolen cashpoint machine to fleece cardholders, but the British case involved the first homemade dispenser in a crime of this sort. The most sophisticated component of the fraud was a magnetic card reader, which took information from customers' cards and down-loaded it to a hidden computer.

From that computer it was transmitted via a modem to the gang's headquarters, along with the electronically recorded PINs. Details were then programmed on to bogus cards.

None of the money has been traced.

BURGLARS NO MATCH FOR MILITARY MIGHT

HONG KONG - Four burglars who targeted houses on Stone-cutter's Island in Hong Kong harbor never had a chance after incurring the wrath of the military.

The houses the burglars raided were the homes of members of the British military garrison in Hong Kong, including Lieutenant-Colonel Nick Southward, who was not impressed when he returned home to find his refrigerator missing.

After another break-in the following night, the garrison stepped up security. "Lo and behold they were stupid enough to come back a third night," said garrison spokesman Roger Goodwin.

One thief was caught trying to sail away with loot in a sampan. His three partners in crime fled into the interior of the island only to find themselves the focus of a military manhunt.

The army sent in Gurkha soldiers by helicopter to boost the search party to 140 and, aided by sniffer dogs, they drove the burglars into the hands of police.

"They must have been the worst-informed criminals in Hong Kong," said Goodwin. "If it's one thing any army has got it's manpower."

Death

SIX DROWN SAVING CHICKEN

CAIRO - Six people, including four from the same family, drowned when they jumped into a well to save a chicken in south Egypt, al-Ahram newspaper reported.

The daily said the chicken had fallen into a farmer's well in the village of Nazlet Emara in Sohag province.

The farmer's 18-year-old son quickly dived in to try to save it but slipped and drowned. His two brothers and sister, aged 20, 16 and 14 respectively, jumped in one after the other to save him but all met the same fate, the paper added.

Two neighbors who came to the siblings' rescue also drowned. A police team which removed the corpses from the well found the chicken alive and floating in the water.

HONEY, NEXT TIME LET'S SHOOT OURSELVES

TAIPEI - A Taiwanese couple failed to jump to their deaths in their third suicide bid in a month, a police officer said.

The couple, only identified as Huang and Chang, jumped hand-in-hand from the 12th story of a hotel in the southern port of Kaohsiung.

The couple refused to say anything after fire fighters rescued them from the roof of a restaurant next to the hotel.

"Their friends said this is the third time in one month that they had tried to commit suicide," the officer added.

The couple had previously tried to commit suicide by driving

their car over a cliff and hanging themselves because their families disapproved of their relationship, local newspapers quoted
friends of the couple as saying.

DEATH, WHERE IS THY STING?

BLANTYRE, Malawi - Mourners attending a funeral in Malawi
stripped off their clothes, fell to the ground unconscious or fled
when a swarm of angry African bees attacked their procession,
the Malawi News reported.

The headman in Thyolo district, near Blantyre, said the bees
attacked about 200 people at the funeral of a 98-year-old
woman. Mourners fled in every direction. A group of women
stripped naked to brush off the bees and 20 people were left
unconscious.

"Nobody was interested to go back to the graveyards to bury
the body until six young men volunteered to go back in the
evening," he was quoted as saying.

CREMATORIUM CATCHES FIRE

SAN ANTONIO, Texas - A crematorium caught fire after funeral
home workers loaded a 400-pound body on top of another
body already inside the furnace, firefighters said.

"Can you overload those? I don't know," said San Antonio

District Fire Department Chief Rodney Hitzfelder, who ruled the fire accidental.

A body was in the burning unit at Woodlawn Memorial Park in San Antonio when workers loaded another body "400 pounds or over" into the furnace for cremation, Hitzfelder said.

"They're not sure whether that contributed to the overheating or not," he said.

"The (workers) left the premises, which is normal, because it takes several hours for a body to be cremated. The unit malfunctioned and caught some nearby combustibles on fire, destroying the building," Hitzfelder said.

No one was injured in the fire, which investigators said caused an estimated $125,000 in damages.

GRANDMOTHER DROWNS IN BARREL

BUDAPEST, Hungary - A grandmother fell into a barrel and drowned in cabbage juice while making lunch for her three-year-old great grandson in eastern Hungary, a newspaper said.

The child's crying alerted neighbors to the accident on Sunday in the town of Ebes, where the woman, who was in her 80s and was from the Transylvania region of Romania, was visiting relatives, the Nepszabadsag newspaper said.

The woman lost her balance in the kitchen and fell into a cabbage barrel. She drowned in liquid which had seeped from the stored cabbage leaves.

CHATTERBOX WIFE MURDERS HUSBAND WHO HID PHONE

LONDON - A talkative wife who killed her husband after he hid the telephone to stop her using it was jailed for four years.

The woman admitted the manslaughter of her husband, who could not tolerate the time she spent on the phone, London's Old Bailey court was told.

She stormed out of her London house when he hid the phone. Returning two days later, she stabbed him with a kitchen knife.

Defense lawyers said she suffered frequent beatings by her drunken husband who once hit her so hard that he broke her jaw.

EXPLODING PIG INJURES FARMER

CLUJ, Romania - A Romanian farmer was injured when a pig which he had slaughtered for his Christmas dinner exploded.

A doctor who treated the farmer's wounds at Cluj, in Transylvania, told Reuters the man had inflated the dead pig with butane gas to make it easier to clean the skin.

Transylvanians traditionally eat pork at Christmas and treat the rind as a delicacy. Farmers inflate the pig using the exhaust of a vacuum cleaner or a pump to tighten the skin and burn straw to remove the hair and clean it.

The farmer's cleaner was broken so he used bottled gas. The pig exploded when he singed its hairs with a naked flame.

The blast tore the pig to pieces and hurled its owner to the ground. He spent three days in the hospital recovering.

MIX-UP LEAVES GRIEVING SON TALKING TO WRONG ASHES

LONDON - A grieving son who has spent two months talking to ashes he thought were those of his dead mother has been told her remains are still at the crematorium.

"Who have I been talking to for the past seven weeks if it wasn't my mum?" the 51-year-old bachelor was quoted as saying in the Sun newspaper.

The Sun said the crematorium told the man the ashes of his late mother would be scattered unless he claimed them. They have not revealed whose remains he received by mistake.

"Some people have told me just to dump them on the roses, but I can't do that," he said.

AT LEAST HE'S NOT IN PRISON . . .

ALBENGA, Italy - The family of an Italian man who lay dead in his bathtub for years assumed he was in prison, police said.

The decomposed body of the 36-year-old man was discovered in the apartment where he lived alone, the ANSA news agency said.

A medical examiner determined that Ligato, whom investigators believe was asphyxiated by a faulty gas heater, might have been dead for nearly four years. A betting slip dated January 1988 was found in his pocket.

Police said there had been no family inquiries about the man, who had been arrested several times on minor charges, ANSA reported.

"We thought he was in prison," an unidentified family member was quoted as saying.

SUNBATHER BAKES TO DEATH

LONDON - A man baked himself to death while sunbathing on a remote British beach during a heatwave, police said.

The man, in his 40s and wearing shoes and shorts, was found in "severe distress" on a remote nudist beach near Hastings, in southern England.

"A post mortem examination will be carried out today to establish the exact cause of the death," a police spokesman in Hastings said. 'The indication is that he died of severe sunburn and there are not thought to be any suspicious circumstances."

Temperatures have soared above 80 degrees this week across Britain, which is above the average and far warmer than recent cool, cloudy weather.

The man, who has not been named, was dead on arrival at the hospital.

GRAVEYARD NOT FOR EVERY TOM, DICK AND HARRY

LONDON - An English vicar who said "dad" and "granddad" were too undignified to appear on tombstones in his church-yard has provoked another row by banning abbreviated names, newspapers reported.

Rev. Stephen Brian, who returned from holiday to find 'Tom Dixon" on a headstone erected in his absence, told masons to replace it with one bearing the man's full name, Thomas John Dixon.

Dixon's widow Olive, 64, who was also asked to foot the fresh bill of several hundred pounds accused the vicar of being cruel, insensitive and ridiculous.

"Who is Thomas? Not my husband. I would be placing my flowers on the grave of a stranger," she said. "In nearly 40 years of marriage I only ever called him Tom."

Earlier this month Brian, vicar of Holy Trinity Church in the village of Freckleton in Lancashire, northwest England, won the backing of a church court over his ban on familiar terms.

Newspapers said the children of the dead man at the center of that dispute were considering exhuming his body and bury-ing him elsewhere so they could use the word "Dad" on his memorial.

As a compromise in the latest wrangle, the vicar says he might allow 'Tom" in brackets after the man's full name.

SUICIDES HAPPEN AROUND LUNCH, REPORT SHOWS

LONDON - Suicides are most likely to occur around lunchtime but failed attempts happen most often in the early evening, Italian researchers said.

The researchers said women were twice as likely as men to attempt suicide, but men were twice as likely to succeed.

Writing in the British Medical Journal the researchers reported on their study of 71 men and 141 women who had poisoned themselves in Ferrara, northern Italy, over a three-year period.

The time of the suicide attempt was charted to see if there was a link with biological rhythms. Their results indicated that the risk of attempting suicide was greatest in the early evening. The risk of successful suicide was greatest during the late morning/early afternoon.

SOCCER FAN, UPSET OVER LOSS, KILLS HIMSELF

SHANGHAI, China - Distraught by his team's loss in a cup match, a Chinese soccer fan committed suicide by throwing himself out of a window, Shanghai's Liberation Daily said.

The soccer-crazy 29-year-old, identified only by his surname Jiang, killed himself on July 23 after his favorite team, Shandong Taishan, lost an away game 2-1 to Beijing's Guoan.

Jiang had watched the match live on television in his parent's bedroom, the paper said. Shandong scored first, and it was more than Jiang could bear when Guoan drew level and then scored the winning goal in the last few minutes of the semifinal of the All-China Football Federation Championship.

Jiang, his face shrouded in unhappiness, slowly walked back to his bedroom, locked the door, opened the window and jumped from the fourth floor," the paper said.

He was cremated along with soccer magazines and T-shirts bought by his father.

DISTRAUGHT SALESMAN HURLS HIMSELF INTO PIT OF JAGUARS

GUATEMALA CITY - A Guatemalan gun salesman committed suicide by hurling himself into a pit of jaguars in Guatemala City's zoo after accidentally shooting a customer to death.

The 32-year-old man was rescued from the pit by firefighters who used fire extinguishers to repel four jaguars, but died in a hospital from the mauling, zoo manager Walter Bolanos said.

In a suicide note addressed to a Guatemalan police chief, the man explained that he killed a young woman in his gun shop in an exclusive shopping center in the capital earlier this week while demonstrating how to use a pistol.

"It was an accident, I didn't mean to kill her. I just wanted to sell her the weapon so she could defend herself from criminals," said the suicide note found in his pocket.

WOMAN KILLED BY FALLING MAN

BANGKOK, Thailand - A Danish woman was killed when a man who fell from the 18th floor of a Bangkok building landed on her as she sunbathed by a swimming pool, police said.

The woman was identified by police as Migerzen Molganson, 19. Her home town was not known.

The man who died in the fall was identified by police as Yongyudh Saebei, 47, a Thai national.

Police said it was not known if Yongyudh fell by accident or jumped from the residential condominium in the Thai capital.

PIZZA WORKER KNEADED TO DEATH IN DOUGH MIXER

JERUSALEM - An Israeli soldier on leave from combat duty met his end at Jerusalem's Mystic Pizza when he was sucked into a giant dough mixer and kneaded to death, police said.

The 21-year-old soldier was due to be discharged from the army within days and was working at the restaurant following combat duty in south Lebanon.

A co-worker at the Mystic Pizza said the man had reached into the mixer to pull up dough from the bottom when he was sucked in and crushed.

DO-IT-YOURSELF BURIAL SAVES MONEY

BUCHAREST, Romania - Taking your own shovel to a funeral is the latest way to save money in post-communist Romania, according to sensational broadsheet Evenimentul Zilei.

"Bring your own gravediggers and save money," the newspaper said in a front-page story about the high cost of dying in Bucharest. It said city cemeteries were allowing burial parties to bury their own to avoid the fees of state gravediggers.

In a city where it is not uncommon to see coffins being carried on car roof racks or even on trams, families were apparently digging graves themselves to avoid a charge which, depending on the cemetery's status, can rise to $35.

City burial officials denied they were allowing freelancers into their plots.

Said Bucharest city cemetery technical director Cristian Stefanescu: "We don't let amateurs dig graves in our cemeteries."

SOME BODY MISSING AT THE FUNERAL

BAD REICHENHALL, Germany - An undertaker drove 560 miles to a funeral before realizing that he had forgotten the body, German border police said.

The man was driving a hearse to a burial in Zagreb, Croatia, from a morgue in the west German town of Bottrop when a colleague pointed out his oversight in a telephone conversation at the German-Austrian border.

The driver immediately turned around to pick up the coffin.

BARKING UP THE WRONG FAMILY TREE

LONDON - An amateur historian spent 30 years tracing his family tree, only to be told he was studying the wrong one because he had been adopted, Britain's Daily Star newspaper said.

"It was 30 years work for nothing," said the British restaurant owner.

On his quest, the 43-year-old man traveled all over Britain and talked to 2,000 relatives. He even planned to write a book about how his great-grandfather left to seek his fortune in Russia and how his grandfather was expelled after the revolution and returned to Britain.

But his search ended when his cousin's wife told him he was adopted and he then traced the adoption papers, the newspaper reported. Both his real and adoptive parents are now dead.

Despite the disappointment, he said he had not lost his taste for family trees. "I will have to start again, but I am determined to carry on," he said.

GOLFER HOLES OUT, THEN DIES

WELLINGTON, New Zealand - A 73-year-old New Zealand golfer scored the first hole-in-one of his life but died a few hours later, the New Zealand Press Association reported.

The man scored his ace at the Queen's Park Golf Club in Southland, in the south of New Zealand, where he was playing in a local competition and was later presented with a hole-in-one tie.

He collapsed on his arrival home and died shortly after. The cause of his death was not immediately known.

TOURIST SPENDS NIGHT WITH CORPSE

MIAMI - A German tourist who complained to Miami hotel keepers about a foul odor in his room unknowingly spent the night sleeping in a bed that concealed a corpse police said.

The badly decomposed body of an unidentified woman was found under the bed in room 202 at the hotel near Miami International Airport, police detective Ralph Fernendez said.

A maid discovered the corpse while investigating the guest's complaint about a horrible smell in his room. The unidentified German visitor is not a suspect in the woman's death and was allowed to return to his homeland, police said.

POET IS DENIED HIS POUND OF FLESH

EUGENE, Oregon - Oregon poet Donal Eugene Russell won't get his last wish—to be skinned so that his hide could be used as a cover for a volume of his poetry.

His widow, Rachel Barton-Russell, settled a lawsuit brought by the state of Oregon, agreeing to have her late husband cremated.

Russell, who died in February at the age of 62, left instructions in his will that the skin from his body was to be removed and tanned and then used to bind a volume of his works.

Barton-Russell, a 33-year-old law student at the University of Oregon, was prepared to honor the terms of the will by letting some friends and expert animal skinners remove the skin from the corpse which had been kept in a freezer.

"He was very fond of his skin. He felt like it was one of his better attributes and he really wanted it used this way," she told reporters last week after the state went to court to block the action.

Russell died in February on his way to a doctor's appointment.

MAN MURDERS MOM, THEN TAKES HER FOR A DRIVE

TOKYO - A man found driving around with his dead mother in the back seat claimed he had strangled her and just wanted to take her for a final spin, Japanese police said.

Police stopped the man after reports he had been driving in a bizarre fashion through the city of Nagoya in the middle of the night.

Then they discovered the body of his 71-year-old mother.

The befuddled man, who earlier had apparently swallowed several sleeping pills, told police the old woman had suffered from a heart condition for the past five years. He said he had grown tired of looking at her, so he strangled her.

Why did he take her out for a drive? "I was trying to give her a final memory to take with her to the netherworld," he added.

A REALLY STUPID WAY TO DIE

ZURICH, Switzerland - A 20-year-old Swiss was killed when he leaned out of a train door in a craze called "train surfing" and struck his head against a signal, police said.

The man, who was not named, opened the door as the train was traveling at 60 miles an hour from Zurich to a nearby town.

He held on to a side grip with his hands and leaned away from the train but hit his head against a signal post and fell to the side of the track. A guard stopped the train but the man was already dead.

It was Switzerland's third death from train surfing, which has also claimed victims in other countries.

ROMANIANS TAKE CORPSE BY TRAIN TO SAVE FUNERAL COSTS

BUCHAREST, Romania - Three Romanians sat their dead uncle's corpse upright on a railway seat for a 300-mile journey to the family graveyard because they could not afford to rent a hearse.

A reporter from the daily Adevarul who was on the train for the bizarre journey said the relatives doused the clothed body with cheap alcohol to conceal the smell and told the conductor their uncle was drunk.

They took the night train for the trip from Bucharest to their 50-year-old uncle's native area of Caransebes in western Romania, because carrying the body in a hearse would have cost 30 times more than a train ticket.

The scheme worked because the train—like most in Romania—was unheated and had no lights.

MAN'S SUICIDE ALSO KILLS HIS NEIGHBOR

PITTSBURGH - A man who used carbon monoxide to commit suicide inadvertently killed his neighbor when the fumes from his garage entered her apartment.

Police in Chartiers Township, a Pittsburgh suburb, said the 35-year-old man died as he sat in his car with the engine running in the garage of his apartment.

They said the fumes apparently entered the apartment of his 86-year-old neighbor and killed her as she sat in a rocking chair in her bedroom.

The bodies were discovered over the weekend. Autopsies confirmed that both died of carbon monoxide poisoning, officials said.

Washington County Coroner Timothy Warco ruled the man's death a suicide and the woman's an accident.

Love and Marriage

TAICHUNG, TAIWAN, 14 JAN 96 - Taiwanese groom Lee Wong-tsong (R) pretends to relieve himself while his bride, Chiu Chiu-kuei, looks on and smiles during the couple's wedding cere-mony staged inside a bathroom designed by Chiu and built by Lee January 14 in the central city of Taichung. Photo by Simon Kwong   REUTERS

THE BRIDE WORE WHITE; SO DID THE TOILETS

TAICHUNG, Taiwan - Eight Taiwan couples got married inside a luxurious one-million-dollar public lavatory that one of the couples had designed and built.

Bride Chiu Chiu-kuei designed the toilets, set in a public park in the central city of Taichung, and her groom, Lee Wong-tsong, built them.

"Since the bathroom is the creation of me and my husband it is very meaningful to us and therefore we decided to have our ceremony in here," Chiu said.

The couple said the lavatory, complete with elaborate decoration, had cost about one million dollars to build.

Chiu and Lee also celebrated their engagement at the lavatory. They said they had chosen the unusual site for the festivities because it was the place everyone visits most often.

MARRIAGE WITH STRINGS ATTACHED

LONDON - A British man, besotted for 35 years, has finally "married" the object of his desire - his guitar.

Chris Black, 53, says he fell for his Fender Stratocaster the moment he saw it. "We've had such a long engagement that I decided it was time we did the decent thing," Black said.

Black asked a friend to perform the wedding ceremony last weekend after a local vicar refused to do it.

"It was all over in a matter of minutes. We didn't even have time for a honeymoon," Black told the UK News.

Not surprisingly his wife of 29 years, Janet, is less than impressed. "My wife thinks I'm crazy," said Black who is unrepentant. "When I die, I want to be buried with it."

SETTLEMENT, SCHMETTLEMENT!

MOSCOW - A man blew up his former house in the former Soviet republic of Moldova after a court awarded it to his ex-wife in a divorce settlement, Itar-Tass news agency said.

It said the couple had a row in the house and the ex-wife ran out. The man, who had drunk a glass of vodka, then opened a gas tap in the kitchen and threw a lighted match into it.

The man emerged from the debris bruised but without serious injury, although a passer-by's leg was broken when a wall collapsed, Tass said.

LACK OF LOVE NO BASIS FOR DIVORCE

MADRID, Spain - Lack of love is no reason to get a divorce, a Spanish appeals court has ruled.

The court in Pontevedra, in Spain's northern Galicia region, threw out a divorce case on the basis that the mere absence of love did not legally justify a couple splitting, Spanish television reported.

The television said the court also dismissed the fact that the couple, from the nearby port of Vigo, had been living apart for a year and that one of them had complained of threats from the other.

"JUDAS KISS" COSTS ADULTEROUS LOVER HIS TONGUE

RIO DE JANEIRO, Brazil - A jealous woman punished her lover in Brazil after she found out he was married by biting off a chunk of his tongue while pretending to kiss him, police said.

'The woman swallowed the piece of tongue to prevent him from having it sewn back on," said a police spokesman in the northeastern city of Salvador.

The attack occurred after the woman found out her lover was married, police said.

The man is recovering in hospital.

'That was a real Judas kiss," the man, unable to speak, wrote on a piece of paper, police said. He was referring to disciple Judas Iscariot's kissing Jesus Christ after betraying him to the Romans.

The woman has disappeared, police said.

ROMEO WALKS ON KNEES IN VAIN FOR LOVE

SAO PAULO, Brazil - A love-struck Brazilian artist, distraught over the breakup of a four-year relationship with his girlfriend, walked nine miles on his knees in a bid to win back her love.

Unimpressed, she still rejected him.

Shuffling along with pieces of car tire tied to his kneecaps and cheered on by motorists and passers-by, the 21-year-old artist took 14 hours to complete his marathon of love from Praia Grande to Santos on the Sao Paulo coast.

The gesture was in vain. When he arrived, exhausted, at her home, his 19-year-old former girlfriend had left to avoid seeing him.

"All I want is for her to come back to me," the artist said.

JILTED MAN ADVERTISES FOR HONEYMOON STAND-IN

LONDON - A jilted British bridegroom is advertising for a female companion to share his pre-booked honeymoon holiday in Barbados after his fiancee broke off their relationship.

The 52-year-old car dealer placed an advertisement in the Times newspaper offering to share the two-week Caribbean holiday for free with a "feminine" woman aged between 25 and 45 after being ditched by his girlfriend Barbara, the Sun tabloid reported.

"I don't want to waste the trip but I couldn't bear to go to

Barbados alone," the Sun, part of the same publishing group as the Times, quoted him as saying.

He said he did not expect the chosen candidate to share his bed but added "it is a honeymoon and it would be lovely if we got close." Fifty women have so far answered the advertisement.

MAN, 100, MARRIES GIRL, 12

KAMPALA, Uganda - A 100-year-old Ugandan man married a 12-year-old girl after an affair that lasted for months, a Ugandan newspaper reported.

The Monitor said that the man, a witch doctor, was married to the girl in a traditional ceremony in the western Rubazi village on July 1.

Ugandan laws do not permit marriage or even sexual affairs with girls under 18 years and the offense is normally punishable by life imprisonment. But the groom insisted he would keep his bride despite opposition from the child's parents and villagers, The Monitor said.

LETTER TAKES SIX YEARS TO ARRIVE

ATHENS, Greece - Antonia Hatzakis sent a message to her fiancee in June 1987 telling him she was expecting a baby. The letter finally reached him this week, and it was opened by the little boy with whom she had been pregnant.

In the six years and eight months it took the letter to travel 90 miles between the towns of Chania and Iraklion on the Greek island of Crete, Antonia had married her fiancee and given birth to the child.

The envelope was opened by the couple's six-year-old son.

The post office said it could not explain the delay.

"We often wondered what happened to that letter," Antonia's husband Manolis Hatzakis told reporters. "Better late than never."

Sex

PRISON NO PLACE FOR A SEX DOLL, COURT SAYS

JERUSALEM - Israel's Supreme Court has burst an Israeli prisoner's dream of having an inflatable sex doll in his cell.

In a ruling appearing in the Israeli media, the court accepted the argument of prison authorities that the 35-year-old inmate could use a doll to fool guards in an escape attempt or hide drugs in it.

The Prison Service also contended other inmates would fight over the doll.

"I've been in jails since the age of 14. If they let me be with a woman, I would give up on getting a doll," said the inmate, imprisoned this time for 10 years for what newspapers described as acts of violence.

HAIR SALON TAKES A BIT OFF THE TOP

ADELAIDE, Australia - A visit to a certain barbershop in this South Australian city is a hair-raising experience in more ways than one— Fiona's Mensworld Hair Design has gone topless.

It's a novelty, but I think it's going to work," said manager Jim, who declined to give his last name. "There's topless restaurants and topless bars, so why not topless hair salons?"

The service is for adults only and a hands-off rule will be strictly enforced, Jim said.

He interviewed about 30 potential topless cutters and hired two.

"There were no real requirements except that they were experienced haircutters. . . . The people that applied knew what we were after."

A topless trim does not come cheap. Jim is paying his cutters triple their normal salary and charging clients double the old price to revive his flagging business.

THE NAKED CZECH IS IN THE MAIL

PRAGUE, Czech Republic - The Czech post office is investigating how fake stamps showing frontal male nudes slipped the attention of clerks and were duly franked with official postmarks.

"Czech Post Office Stamps Penises," said a front-page headline in the mass-circulation Blesk newspaper, which also ran a photo of the stamp.

Blesk said it had received a spate of anonymous letters with the fake stamps.

"These are clippings of naked men taken from some magazine, and then stuck in the place of the stamp," Blesk editor Robert Sobota said.

"The remarkable thing is that the post office . . . postmarked these filthy things," he said.

CANNES, FRANCE, 23 MAY 95 - French adult pornographic film star Lolo Ferrari, who claims to have the largest breasts in Europe, stands near the "Hot d'Or" statue, May 23. The best pornographic film actress will receive the winged statue during a ceremony Wednesday May 24, as the Cannes International Film Festival continues. Photo by Eric Gaillard REUTERS

THEY'RE GETTING TOO HOT IN THE SAUNA

HELSINKI, Finland - A sports center near Helsinki which tried to introduce a mixed sauna has had to wall off the sexes after some men failed to contain their ardor, the management said.

The experiment was rare in Finland, home of the sauna where the sexes are usually strictly segregated and always bathe nude.

"We thought, if they can be mixed in central Europe, why not in Finland?" ' Kirsi-Marja Mustakari, a manager at the center in Toolo, said. "Unfortunately, a few men could not control themselves."

When the few first became a nuisance, the center put up a low wall, she said.

But they hopped over it, so a higher barrier had to be built.

"The wall is made of glass so you can see through it- the idea is just to stop the minority of men who seek skin contact," Mustakari said. Even so, some men have complained and others have tried to scale the new barrier.

STRIPTEASER CHARMS CAPTIVE AUDIENCE

MOSCOW - Margarita from Siberia is beating the Soviet economic crisis by stripping for prisoners at a labor camp overlooked by her home in Krasnoyarsk.

Inmates exercising in the camp compound throw bundles up

to her balcony containing money and instructions on when she should appear and take off her clothes.

"During the summer I got 100 rubles a time, but I put my price up in the autumn. That's inflation for you," 30-year-old Margarita told the newspaper Komsomolskaya Pravda. "Some months I earned five or six thousand rubles."

The average Soviet monthly wage is just over 300 rubles.

But Margarita's lucrative work has been interrupted by the first snow of the Siberian winter.

"It's seasonal work," she explained. "In winter it gets cold on the balcony and the windows freeze so they can't see anything through the glass."

THE NUDES ARE ON AISLE SIX

AMSTERDAM - Dutch police are hunting a gang of supermarket robbers who rely on female accomplices stripping to create a distraction while they strike.

Dutch news agency ANP said the striptease gang had staged three successful heists in the towns of Zwolle and Groningen, but that a third attempt in Zwolle had failed.

Shoppers and staff looked on in amazement as the women peeled off their clothes and it was only when the tumult had died down that store managers realized they had been robbed.

GOLDILOCKS: THE ADULT VERSION

BOSSIER CITY, Louisiana - A teenage couple who decided to try out a bed in a department store were arrested for obscenity after a customer complained to the manager that the two were having sex in public.

Bossier City police spokesman Mike Halphen said that a 19-year-old youth and his 17-year-old girlfriend each face up to six months in jail and a $500 fine on the obscenity charge.

A customer at Dillard's department store in Bossier City complained to the manager about noon that two young people were having sex on a daybed in the furniture department, police said.

The manager went to the department, saw the same thing and called police. When officers arrived the couple was sitting on the daybed.

"They admitted what they had done, apologized, and said they knew it was wrong and they shouldn't have done it," Halphen said.

"I consider myself a man of the world, but never would I have expected this in Dillard's," he said chuckling.

PROSTITUTION SPURS BUSINESS IN 'RESTORING' VIRGINITY

HANOI, Vietnam - Some businessmen pay so much for sex with Vietnamese virgins in Ho Chi Minh City that it's spawned a new business—surgical virginity "restoration."

The Nguoi Lao Dong (Worker) newspaper said some foreigners were prepared to pay up to $3,000 a night to sleep with a virgin.

Many so-called beauty parlors had made a lot of money from "restoring virginity to unfortunate girls," the newspaper said.

Growing numbers of single girls were temporarily going into prostitution, then spending $100 to $150 for surgery before getting married.

"Many young girls believe that they can feel safe to indulge themselves in these sex adventures because when they need to turn a new leaf in their lives, the virginity can be rehabilitated painlessly," the newspaper said.

Other prostitutes have the surgery so they can be passed off as virgins to customers more than once.

The daily said the fake beauty parlors were partly to blame for "the undermining of the social virtue down to the level of perverseness and decline."

SOLDIERS SPRING SEX TRAP ON COMMANDER

JERUSALEM - For sex-starved soldiers at an Israeli base, revenge can be sweet—or at least diverting.

Troops irked by an order segregating male and female soldiers after dark set a sex trap at the weekend for the woman commander who enforced the directive, the newspaper Maariv said.

"In a scene reminiscent of the film 'M*A*S*H'," the newspaper said, "the soldiers sent one of their number to seduce her and have intimate relations with her in his barracks while they spied on the act."

An army spokesman, without confirming or denying specifics of the incident, said the case was under investigation. He said the woman commander, an officer and three other soldiers would stand trial.

The newspaper said the soldiers, "equipped with chairs and ladders" for a better view of the military love nest, broke into song and dance after having watched the goings-on for a long time.

The base commander then arrived, causing the troops to flee so fast that one fell off a roof and broke his leg, Maariv said.

As for the couple, "this morning she and her partner are to stand trial, charged with unlawful loitering in opposite-sex barracks, and disturbing the peace and discipline of the army."

AND THEY DIDN'T EVEN HAVE TO
PAY FOR CABLE

BEIJING - Television viewers in China's Henan province were jolted out of their seats recently when a regularly scheduled soap opera was suddenly interrupted by an hour and a half of hard-core pornography, the official Beijing Youth News said.

The incident occurred in Henan's Dancheng city on March 10, when the late-evening soap "Crazy Hong Kong" was inadvertently replaced with a sex video.

"Because of lax internal administration at the television station, somebody used the machinery to record pornography over the soap opera. Workers on duty did not turn it off immediately," the newspaper said.

It said that after the surprise interruption the Dancheng city authorities ordered the suspension of the director and deputy director of the television station and the head of the municipal broadcast administration.

DARK AND DIRTY WORK - SOMEBODY
HAS TO DO IT

LONDON - Undercover council officials and police were accused of being overzealous when they felt it necessary to visit a massage parlor 17 times to see if it was breaking British law.

Labor councilor Ben Summerskill said they went "beyond the

call of duty" with visits that cost a total of close to 2,000 pounds ($3,160).

The inspectors said they were given "amateurish massages" by scantily clad young women before being offered full sex.

They politely refused and left.

The north London parlor has not had its license renewed by Westminster Council, whose officers argued that the 17 visits were needed to prove it was the owner and not individual masseuses who were breaking the law.

Animals

COO! THIS IS MY STOP! COO!

LONDON - Readers of New Scientist magazine have started a debate over whether Pigeons are using London's metro system to get about the capital. In letters to Friday's edition, several said they had noticed birds hopping on and off underground trains—apparently deliberately.

One reader reported seeing a pair of pigeons getting on a train at one station, Aldgate, staying by the door, and "alighting with purpose" at the next, Tower Hill. "How did they know the platform for Tower Hill was the same side of the carriage as that for Aldgate?" she asked.

Another reader, noting pigeons have renowned navigational facilities, wrote: "I see no reason why they should not have cottoned on to the fact that travel by tube saves their wings."

DOG RESCUED AFTER CLIFF PLUNGE

LONDON - A dog survived a 100-foot plunge over a Cornish cliff and two weeks of pounding surf to be returned to its owner, British newspapers reported.

They carried pictures of Judy, a sandy-colored mongrel who was stranded at the bottom of the cliff and hauled up howling by rescuers after she was spotted by bird-watchers.

She had fallen over the cliff at St Just in Cornwall 14 days ago, newspapers quoted owner Dave Holden as saying.

Coastguards searched for more than an hour but decided the dog, who was not used to the rough Cornish countryside, must be dead.

"She's skinnier and looks a bit sorry for herself, but otherwise she's as good as new," Holden said.

"She was spotted on Monday afternoon and it took our team of six rescuers two hours to get her to the top of the cliff," a spokesman for Falmouth coastguard said.

DOG LOVER DIES, IS EATEN BY HUNGRY PETS

NEW YORK - An elderly dog lover who died of natural causes in her New York home earlier this week was eaten from the waist down by the 18 malnourished dogs she left behind, police said.

The mutilated body was found near the front door of her two-story home in Queens, police said.

She had been eaten from the waist down by the eighteen dogs roaming around her home, which was littered with canine feces, covered in cobwebs and devoid of all furniture, including a mattress.

The woman, who was in her eighties, had died earlier in the week from natural causes, a spokeswoman from the medical examiner's office said.

The dogs, all various mixed breeds, who were found suffering from malnutrition and mange were being cared for by animal welfare officials.

JAKE THE DRUG-BUST DOG ABDUCTED

DUBLIN - Irish police are still looking for a lead on who abducted one of the country's top drug-busters—Jake the sniffer dog.

Some believe the captors who snatched Jake from his home at the weekend were well aware of the golden Labrador's success rate.

He has nosed out drugs worth more than 14 million dollars over six years, mainly at the ferry port of Rosslare.

Jake was stolen from his handler's house in County Wexford by thieves who used wirecutters to get to his compound through a perimeter fence.

ARMY SNIFFER DOGS TO GET BOOTS

LONDON - The British Army, tackling an Irish guerrilla bombing campaign in London, is to issue sniffer dogs with special protective boots, a military spokesman said.

The boot-wearing dogs, trained to sniff out arms and explosives, will be able to explore bombed buildings without lacerating their paws on metal and glass fragments, said spokesman Dennis Barnes.

The new rip-proof boots are being tested by Sam and Luke, two black Labradors. "They look like a diver's wet suit. The dogs appear quite happy with them," Barnes told Reuters.

FISH PRICE DROPS OVER FEAR OF CORPSES

JAKARTA, Indonesia - The price of large fish in the north Sumatran town of Banda Aceh has dropped on fears the fish may be feeding on the corpses of 100 people still missing from a ferry disaster last week, Antara news agency said.

The ferry Gurita sank on January 19 with 210 people on board. Only 40 people survived and 54 bodies were recovered.

"It seems the people of Banda Aceh are reluctant to buy large ocean fish because they worry the fish have already eaten the corpses of people who died . . . ," the official news agency quoted a housewife, Halimah, 40, as saying.

BAN ON CHIMP ADS SOUGHT

SAO PAULO, Brazil - Brazil's environmental protection institute said it would try to ban television advertisements promoting beer and soda sales by showing chimpanzees driving Jeeps and swilling beer and soft drinks amid throngs of bikini-clad women.

"Driving a car and drinking beer or soda is not a monkey's natural habitat," said Lilian Daher, a spokeswoman for the government's environmental institute Ibama.

An Ibama attorney will ask a Sao Paulo judge to block the airing of all ads showing chimpanzees in unnatural surroundings, Daher said.

The ads violated a constitutional ban on exploiting wild animals and could encourage the traffic in endangered species by making the idea of having a pet chimp seem more attractive, she said.

Since mid-January, Brazilian television viewers have been treated to a barrage of soda and beer ads in what one Brazilian news weekly has dubbed "Monkeymania."

Most of the ads feature a chimp, dressed for the beach, who is able to woo beautiful women with his playful antics and ability to guzzle a particular brand of soda or beer.

MAN REVIVES PET DOG WITH KISS OF LIFE

SYDNEY, Australia - An Australian has proven that man is a dog's best friend, by giving his terrier the kiss of life.

Journalist Lindsay Tuffin, commenting on local media reports of his extraordinary feat, said he acted out of impulse when he wrapped his mouth across his pet Katie's muzzle and "just breathed straight down her throat."

He even gave her heart massage as Katie, strangled by her own collar, lay motionless and apparently dead on the Tuffin family's verandah, its dog tag caught between the deck's wooden planks.

"Much to my astonishment and great relief, after a minute or so, her eyes flickered and her body trembled and gradually she came around," he told Reuters by telephone from the southern city of Hobart.

"She's been looking at me with extremely fond eyes ever since."

RACEHORSE GOES FOR RUN ON HIGHWAY

TOKYO - A stray racehorse went for a two-mile trot along a Tokyo highway near Haneda airport before it stopped at a toll-gate and was caught by police.

Police said the three-year-old filly, Super Otome (girl), got onto the highway after running away from a stable at Oi race-course, located on Tokyo Bay.

A Metropolitan Expressway Public Corporation official called police after seeing the horse on a monitor screen. Hundreds of calls were also received by car drivers.

The filly was unhurt and no traffic accidents were caused by its unscheduled run, police said.

UNIVERSITY TO INVESTIGATE OKAPI BARBECUE RUMORS

COPENHAGEN, Denmark - University officials in Denmark be-gan an investigation of media reports that students held a bar-becue party serving up the meat of an okapi which had died of shock in Copenhagen zoo after hearing an operatic concert.

The rare, cud-chewing, giraffelike African okapi threw a fit, collapsed and died last month in the zoo, killed by the noise of Wagnerian music played at a nearby open-air opera concert given by the Royal Danish Orchestra.

After its death, the five-year-old okapi was sent to Copenhagen University's Zoological Museum for skinning for research purposes, mammal section chief Hans Baagoe said.

He was unable to confirm the media reports that students last week stole the meat and cooked it at a barbecue party, but promised a full investigation.

The okapi, a mammal, is sensitive to unusual noises. In Africa it is a protected species.

HARD-HEARTED ROBBERS SHOW SOFT SPOT FOR FAMILY DOG

BRADFORD, England - Robbers held a terrified family at gunpoint for 10 hours but could not bear to see their captives' dog suffer and made sure it was fed before they fled.

Police said they were hunting two armed men who held postmaster Paul Carter and his relatives for a night but left biscuits and water in the morning for the family dog Sheeba.

"They put us through the most awful night and I thought they were going to kill us. I just can't believe they did all that and then fed the dog," Carter told reporters. "It seems they must have a streak of kindness somewhere after all."

The robbery began at night but the thieves decided to wait until morning because the safe at Carter's post office in Bradford, northern England, was on a time-lock. They handcuffed and bound the family and stole about 30,000 pounds ($46,460).

MAN RELIEVES HIMSELF ON DOG, SPARKS PANIC

RIO DE JANEIRO, Brazil - A Rio neighborhood went to the dogs and echoed with the sound of gunfire after a man and a terrier got into a dispute over a call of nature.

The toilet shootout developed when a beer-filled Brazilian student went to relieve himself against a tree, Brazilian news agency Estado reported.

The student mistakenly urinated on a pit bull terrier that was watering the same vegetation and as a result ended up brawling with the dog's owner, Estado said.

When the student's friends chased the owner and his dog to a service station, security guards, thinking a robbery was in progress, fired shots into the air, bringing police rushing to the scene.

After a brief spell behind bars, however, the two men were reported to have made up—over a beer.

SHARK LEAPS INTO BOAT, KILLS FISHERMAN

SUVA, Fiji - A fisherman died after a nine-foot shark leapt into his boat and attacked him while he slept, the state-owned Radio Fiji reported.

The report said the attack took place off Waya Island in the remote Yasawa group.

Local postal agent Timoci Ravouvou told Radio Fiji five men

had been sleeping in the fishing boat, which was anchored in open seas when the attack occurred. He said the shark nearly tore off the right leg and right hand of villager Kinijioji Vindovi, 69, who later died from loss of blood as the other men steered the boat to shore.

AIRLINE STOPS SHEEP-FOR-SLAUGHTER FLIGHTS AFTER PROTESTS

LONDON - British Airways Plc said it was ending flights of live sheep destined for the dinner table after protests from passengers.

"Many of our customers have expressed strong views objecting to the carriage of sheep for slaughter," Robert Ayling, the airline's group managing director, said in a statement.

"I reviewed the matter yesterday . . . including taking account of the animal welfare issues, and we have decided to withdraw from this market," he said.

Animal lovers on board a recent BA flight from Perth to Singapore reacted with shock and revulsion when they found out their flight was being delayed while 40 live Australian sheep, packed into narrow crates, were stowed in the hold.

The sheep were being flown to Singapore where they would be transferred by ship to Saudi Arabia for ritual slaughter.

Among the passengers was member of parliament Sir Teddy Taylor, who wrote to British Airways in protest.

"This is fantastic for animal welfare and I pay tribute to British Airways for having acted so speedily," he said.

The Royal Society for the Prevention of Cruelty to Animals said it had agreed with ferry operator Stena Sealink to work out a code of practice for the transport of livestock.

Stena Sealink promised to make a policy statement by the end of this month. Another ferry company, P&O, has already said it will pull out of the trade by the end of September and Brittany Ferries says it will not carry animals for direct slaughter.

MAN HAD 20 DEAD CATS UNDER HIS BED

HELSINKI, Finland - A Finnish man lived with 20 dead cats under his bed and nearly 30 other ailing cats in his apartment, a newspaper said.

Authorities had to destroy the survivors because of their poor condition, Ilta-Sanomat reported.

A veterinarian and a police officer entered the apartment wearing gas masks to make an inspection ordered by local authorities after reports about the deplorable condition of the man and his pets.

The local sheriff's office was deciding what steps could be taken, the newspaper said, adding that a psychiatrist had found the man to be sane.

CUBAN DOG FINDS U.S. SAFE HAVEN

NEW YORK - Cuban dogs, si. Cuban boat people, no.

A Cuban dog, which joined its master and 11 others on a raft ride across the Straits of Florida, has been granted a safe haven in the United States while the humans who accompanied her have been taken to the U.S. Naval Station at Guantanamo Bay.

A CBS News crew spotted the raft and alerted the Coast Guard which arrived and picked up the humans but refused to take the dog, a female named Diana, saying dogs were not allowed at Guantanamo Bay.

CBS producer Larry Doyle said the Coast Guard's alternative was either to shoot the dog or leave it floating on the raft. "I volunteered to take it and give it to friends and the Coast Guard seemed relieved," Doyle told Reuters.

Since rescuing the dog, CBS said it has been flooded with calls about her welfare. Doyle said that even the Florida Humane Society phoned him to make sure the dog was all right.

"She's better than all right. It turns out she's pregnant and will give birth soon and we have plenty of takers for the pups. But it will be a long time—if ever—until she is reunited with her master," he said.

President Clinton, fearing a huge tide of Cuban refugees, earlier this month reversed longstanding U.S. policy and ordered that all Cubans picked up at sea be taken to the base at Guantanamo rather than allowed entry to the United States.

Doyle said he gave the dog to friends who live in Key West and promised to take good care of her.

LIONESS CATCHES YOUTH WITH PANTS DOWN

MARACAIBO, Venezuela - A lioness attacked and mauled a Venezuelan youth who had hopped into her pen to answer a call of nature.

"I had my trousers around my knees when I heard some growling and saw this ferocious animal hurling itself on top of me," the 19-year-old man said from his hospital bed in this western Venezuelan city.

He wrestled Tarzan-style with the lioness, which sank its claws and teeth into his head and torso "while I just tried to get it off me so I could pull up my trousers."

But he escaped to tell the tale when a quick-thinking friend used a brick to knock out the lioness.

The youth was badly wounded, but well enough to tell a local newspaper how the attack affected his diarrhea.

"It disappeared as if by magic!"

FUGITIVE ALLIGATOR GIVEN REPRIEVE

COLOGNE, Germany - Police hunting Sammy the fugitive alligator roaming a German lake decided to bow to public pressure and stop trying to shoot him.

The three-foot long cayman has gained a fan club since he slipped his leash and dived into the lake at an open-air bathing resort not far from the town of Neuss.

The police, who have been hunting for Sammy with rifles

from pedal boats and dinghies, using blood-soaked steaks as bait, say they will now try to catch him alive.

"We have been overwhelmed by people's sympathy for Sammy," a police spokesman said.

Sammy escaped from his owner, 21-year-old Juergen Zars, and dived into the cooling water to escape a searing heat wave.

"He's really tame," said Zars. "He's even slept in my bed at night."

But experts say the cayman—dubbed 'The Loch Neuss Monster" by German media—can rip through flesh like a shark with his razor-sharp teeth and the resort has been shut while the police search for him.

ANGLERS HUNT FOR DUCK-EATING FISH

STOCKTON-ON-TEES, England - British fishermen are angling for a 30-pound pike nicknamed "Jaws" which has eaten its way through the fish in its lake and has now developed a taste for live duck.

The local authority responsible for the lake in Stockton-on-Tees, northeastern England, said it was lifting a ban on fishing there for two days in the hope that the duck-eating fish will be hooked.

The pike, nicknamed "Jaws" after the film shark that liked human flesh, was meant to keep down fish stocks in the lake but gobbled up the marine life and took a fancy to the ducks.

"This pike seems to have overdone things a bit," John War-brook, chief leisure officer at the town council, told reporters. "We've lost all the ducklings on the lake this year and one of the park staff saw a grown mallard go straight down beneath the water."

POLAR BEAR GIVES FARMER A BATH

BEIJING - A Chinese farmer who jumped into the polar bear enclosure at Beijing Zoo last week was grabbed by one of the huge animals and dipped repeatedly into a pool "like someone washing a chicken," the China Daily said.

Li Rongxing, 24, clambered over a five-yard wall to enter the bear cage saying he wanted to star in a film about the bears, the newspaper said.

"Li began singing and trying to stir them up," the newspaper quoted witnesses as saying.

The female bear ignored the intrusion, but the male grabbed the 21-year old farmer and began dunking him in the wading pool, the paper said.

As onlookers "began shouting and hurling stones," zoo keepers were able to distract the bears and lure them back into their cages. Li was removed from the enclosure with a few scratches and "teeth marks on his buttocks," the paper said.

HOMESTEAD, FL, 21 JAN 96 - Alligators at the Everglades Alligator Farm in Homestead, Florida, bask in the late morning sun January 20. The sunshine state reptile has developed into a multi-million dollar business as licensed farmers generate revenue from the gator's meat and hide. The farms also make popular tourist attractions. About 100,000 Florida alligators are raised on farms and an estimated 1,000,000 are in the wild.   Photo by Colin Braley   REUTERS

KANGAROOS ABOUND IN GOVERNMENT RESIDENCE

CANBERRA, Australia - Vasectomies have failed to stop a troublesome mob of kangaroos from reproducing at the official residence of Australian Governor-General Bill Hayden, the local representative of Britain's Queen Elizabeth.

"It seems female kangaroos can retain a fertilized embryo indefinitely," said Hayden's official secretary, Doug Sturkey, who organized last year's sterilization campaign at Hayden's Canberra residence.

So the mob, the Australian term for a group of kangaroos, grew by nine and now exceeds 60, he said.

Hayden, saying the population growth threatened the gardens, originally wanted to shoot the kangaroos and hold a barbecue.

Ten kangaroos were introduced into the 134-acre grounds in 1984 to amuse visiting foreign dignitaries. But protected from predators and munching on the beautifully manicured lawns, the numbers grew alarmingly, leading to the campaign to sterilize the national symbol.

ARRGH! BOY GROWLS AT BEAR
TO SAVE SISTER

WINNIPEG - A seven-year-old boy became the youngest Canadian ever to win a Medal of Bravery after growling at a black bear attacking his little sister.

"Each time I growled, like this—Arrgh—he took one step back," the Winnipeg boy, Julius Rosenberg, said after the award was announced.

The bear approached as Julius, then five years old, and his three-year-old sister were eating on the dock outside their family's cottage at West Hawk Lake, Manitoba in September, 1992.

They jumped off the dock into the water to escape, but the bear followed, gripping Barbara's life jacket with his jaws as Julius swam to shore.

"He was drowning her," said Julius. "He wanted her to die."

Julius swam back when he heard his sister's cries, tugging her from the bear's grip and pushing her back onto the dock.

But the bear swam to shore and blocked the two children as they tried to run from the dock to the cottage.

"He was by the steps (into the cottage)," said Julius. "When I growled three times he went to the side of the cottage and me and Barbie ran up the steps and closed the door real quick and told my mum."

FOUL-MOUTHED FOWL RUFFLES FEATHERS

LONDON - A blue and gold parrot was sacked from his job at a British zoo after embarrassing parents and children with his foul language.

Bluey, a long-tailed macaw named for his brilliant color and not his explicit language, was part of a six-strong parrot show at the Isle of Wight zoo until he told visitors in no uncertain terms exactly what to do.

"It was no good. We even got in a local elocution teacher, but Bluey told him to go on a sexual excursion too," said Jack Corney, the zoo manager.

"Bluey was previously owned by a sailor. I don't know if that is where he got his bad language from, or somebody has taught him a few naughty words since."

You Have the
Right . . .

GOOD NEWS FOR DISABLED STRIPPERS . . .

LOS ANGELES - A nightclub has been ordered to close down its main attraction, a shower enclosure where nude dancers cavort for male customers, because the enclosure has no wheelchair access.

Los Angeles officials said the club discriminates against wheelchair-bound people because of lack of access to the shower, denying them an equal opportunity to work as nude dancers.

Ron Shigeta, head of the Disabled Access Division of the city's Department of Building and Safety, said the law is the law, no matter how ridiculous it might seem to some people.

"I can't argue one way or the other whether a disabled person would want to be up there performing. But if an able-bodied person could have been up there doing it, a disabled person should have been able to, also," Shigeta told the Los Angeles Daily News.

He said the shower was considered a stage, and a stage had to be accessible to the handicapped.

"They built something that the physically disabled cannot use. The law doesn't allow you to discriminate, and that's what it comes down to, you're denying people the opportunity," he added.

DOPE DEALERS ABLE TO DRAW DOLE

THE HAGUE, The Netherlands - Dealers peddling soft drugs at hundreds of so-called coffee shops throughout the Netherlands are entitled to the same unemployment benefits as ordinary workers, a government advisory body has ruled.

"Dealers who keep to the rules under which sales of soft drugs such as cannabis and marijuana are tolerated should be able to sign on like everyone else," a spokesman for the Social Affairs Ministry said. Drugs are illegal in the Netherlands, but the sale of cannabis is tolerated, making the country's drugs policy one of the most liberal in Europe.

"Everyone who pays their premiums is entitled to unemployment and sickness benefits. There's nothing new about this," the ministry spokesman said.

MENTAL PATIENT KILLS WOMAN, WINS COMPENSATION

LONDON - A paranoid schizophrenic who killed a woman after being released from a hospital mental unit has been awarded compensation after claiming British doctors should never had let him out.

The 40-year-old man was found guilty of manslaughter on the grounds of diminished responsibility after a random knife attack on a woman in Leicester, central England, in 1990.

He was sent to a top security mental hospital, where he is still being treated. Just months before he killed the woman, he had been admitted to a hospital mental ward but was allowed out after psychiatrists ruled he posed no danger to the public.

After he was convicted, he began a legal battle against Leicestershire health authority, claiming it should never have let him out. The health authority said it had made an out-of-court settlement to the man. It declined comment on one report which said the payout was around 30,000 pounds ($47,820).

WOMAN FIRED FOR SWEARING WINS COMPENSATION

AUCKLAND, New Zealand - A New Zealand woman fired from her job in a café because her language was too coarse for patrons from a rugby team won New Zealand $6,240 (US$4,050) in damages from an employment court.

Judge Barrie Travis said in his verdict that the woman had admitted swearing in the kitchen of an establishment called The Café, The Bar and The Casino.

The rugby team, which used the café regularly, told the manager they would take their business elsewhere if her bad language continued. But Travis accepted the explanation that the swearing was not directed at customers but used only in telling dirty jokes or when she cut or burnt herself.

He awarded damages on the grounds the woman had not been served adequate notice of the company's policy on swearing and had been unfairly dismissed.

INMATE SUES JAILERS FOR LOSS OF FLOSS

SAN DIEGO, California - A former inmate is trying to put a financial bite on his jailers because they refused to provide him with dental floss.

Richard Loritz, 31, said he developed four cavities during the three months he was held in the South Bay Detention Facility because he could not floss. He wants to be reimbursed $2,000 for dental expenses.

"Despite several requests, the sheriff's deputies did not provide me with dental floss, which is a medical necessity to prevent cavities," Loritz wrote in a claim.

A former law student, Loritz is accused of shooting his ex-girlfriend six times and is expected to stand trial in three months.

It is against jail policy to give or sell dental floss because it could be used as a weapon, according to jail officials. "We don't even let them have string," an official told a local newspaper.

TOWN CRIER NOT TOO NOISY, COUNCIL DECREES

LONDON - A town crier with a voice as loud as a pneumatic drill has been cleared of noise pollution after merchants complained about his 100-decibel "Oyez, Oyez" calls.

Dave McGuire, celebrating after being cleared by council officials in the city of Chester, said: "You cannot have a quiet town crier. It is a contradiction in terms. You might as well complain that a street cleaner is keeping the road too tidy."

Traders had complained about the bell-ringing McGuire who loudly sang the praises of the local bus company.

"Tests showed he was noisier than a passing bus that registered 85 decibels but no noisier than pneumatic drills which have been measured at 100 decibels," a council spokesman was quoted as saying by the Daily Telegraph newspaper.

FLYING DWARF APPEALS AGAINST GROUNDING

PARIS - A diminutive Frenchman wants the European Court of Human Rights to take action against France for banning the bizarre pastime of "dwarf-throwing."

The 3' 10" man is furious that he has now lost the income—and apparently the enjoyment—he once derived from being hurled around by burly men.

The State Council, France's highest administrative court, ruled last week that dwarf-throwing was degrading to human dignity. Despite complaints by the 28-year-old dwarf, the council upheld bans on the pastime by some local councils.

The man's lawyer said: "Banning him from his work is a restriction of liberty." He said his client, who weighs 97 pounds, had never been injured.

The man has been arguing in favor of dwarf-throwing for

years despite repeated official efforts to ban it as degrading or dangerous.

In a letter to the human rights court he says "This spectacle is my life; I want to be allowed to do what I want."

Dwarf-throwing, imported from the United States and Australia in the 1980s, consists of people throwing a tiny stuntman as far as possible, usually in a bar or discotheque. The human projectile wears a crash helmet and padded clothing which has handles on the back for ease of throwing. The dwarf's flights are usually about six feet long and end on a large inflatable mattress.

MICHELANGELO'S DAVID RULED NOT OBSCENE

HONG KONG - Good news—a Hong Kong judge has ruled that Michelangelo's David is not obscene.

The High Court decision resulted from a case brought by an English-language newspaper, the Eastern Express, which sought to quash a ruling by the colony's Obscene Articles Tribunal that a picture it published of the sculpture was obscene.

The paper's editor said the judge declared no jurist would find the statue of a nude David indecent and referred the case back to the tribunal for a re-ruling.

"Hong Kong is set to become the laughing stock of the world," the paper said when it launched the court case.

LABORER WINS SICK PAY FOR HANGOVER

TORONTO - A laborer who failed to turn up for work because he had too much to drink at a wedding the day before is entitled to sick pay, a Canadian arbitration panel has ruled.

The man's employer, the Metro Toronto Housing Authority, argued that he should not be paid because getting drunk was a "premeditated and self-inflicted condition," the Ontario Grievance Settlement Board said in a report made available to Reuters.

But the board said although there was no dispute the man took the day off in January 1992 because of a hangover, he was entitled to sick leave because he was incapacitated.

". . . It was clear that he had consumed a good deal of alcohol the day previously and that he was in no condition to operate the power equipment he was required to run as part of his duties," the board said.

Its report likened this case of self-inflicted illness to workers who are sick because of lung cancer caused by smoking.

RELIEF AS "PEE BREAK" STRIKE ENDS

PARIS - About 250 relieved workers at a French slaughterhouse ended a strike after a partial victory over their boss's decree that they had to go to the toilet at fixed times or lose pay.

Staff in the "pee break" dispute at the plant in Quimperle, northwest France, were still threatening legal action over restrictions on going to the lavatory outside newly-imposed five-minute breaks, three times a day.

"This dispute sounds like something from the 19th century. We are demanding to go to the toilet according to each person's needs, not at the blow of a whistle. This should be a human right," said a union official.

The three-day strike ended when the plant's owner abandoned a plan to dock $10 from a worker's holiday bonus if he or she spent too long in the washroom or went at the wrong time.

But he was still insisting on fixed breaks for the workers, who cut up beef and pork for packaging. Outside these times, workers would need special permission from bosses.

He said many workers were spending too long socializing at the toilets. Unions say he is merely trying to boost productivity at an already profitable and expanding business.

TRANSSEXUAL INMATE SUES PRISON FOR ESTROGEN

STUART, Florida - A transsexual inmate filed suit against Florida prison authorities claiming they are denying him estrogen treatments needed to match his physical appearance with his inner feelings.

The prisoner who filed the suit identified himself as Rhonda. He said in the court papers he had started hormone treatments at the age of 16, had breast implant surgery and had been married to a man.

But officials at the prison, some 30 miles from Palm Springs, said the inmate had not legally changed his name to Rhonda and they considered him male.

The inmate said his problems began after October 1992, when he was arrested for violating his probation and sent to the Martin Correctional Institution, an all-male maximum security prison.

Authorities during previous incarcerations had allowed him to take the drugs, he said. He was first sent to prison in 1990 on battery charges.

The inmate said his breasts have shrunk, causing discomfort and bruising, he has periods of vomiting, anxiety attacks and fainting spells, since he has been denied the hormone treatments.

"The lack of estrogen has also reversed many of the female characteristics previously attained through treatment," he said in the motion.

These symptoms amount to cruel and unusual punishment, he argued.

SHOUTING TEACHER WINS COMPENSATION

LIVERPOOL, England - A British schoolteacher who lost her voice shouting at her pupils won the right to industrial compensation.

Frances Oldfield, 55, was forced to retire early in January when her voice was reduced to a whisper. Social services officials agreed her voice loss was an industrial injury and promised to pay damages, to be determined later.

Oldfield, who taught primary school students for 17 years in Huyton, northwest England, claimed that the modern "open plan" layout of the school forced her to constantly raise her voice to be heard.

WOMEN-ONLY BUS SERVICE

COLOMBO, Sri Lanka - Sri Lanka launched a women-only bus service in a bid to keep male perverts at bay, transport officials said.

The move follows a survey by the Conference of Public Service Independent Trade Unions which said 81 percent of women complained of some sort of harassment by men while traveling to work on the country's notoriously unsafe and overcrowded buses.

The service uses women drivers and women conductors and will be expanded if there is enough demand.

Medicine

DRUG STOPS STOOL SMELLS

TOKYO - A Japanese company has developed a drug that stops feces from smelling, the Mainichi Daily News reported.

The drug, developed by a Tokyo firm called Dairin, could benefit health care workers by deodorizing the excrement of bedridden patients, the newspaper said.

A patient who took one pill after every meal would have odorless stools, it said.

Called "Etiquette View" the drug is made out of natural ingredients and would be relatively cheap, selling at around 3,000 yen ($30) for 90 pills, the report said.

It quoted Susumu Oda, a professor of psychiatry at Tsukuba University, as being concerned about the possible social effects of such a drug.

He said many Japanese were already obsessed with eliminating dirt and foul odours and some mothers even feared having to change their babies' diapers.

"I wouldn't want to see young people have easy access to them (the pills)," he said.

THRIFTY MAN USES PLIERS ON TOOTH

TENBURY WELLS, England - A hard-up British pensioner balked at spending $32 to have his aching tooth pulled by a dentist and after a glass of whisky at his local pub asked his friend to yank it out with pliers.

Bob Maund, 74, who had suffered three sleepless nights because of the pain, retired to The Vaults pub in Tenbury Wells in central England after finding the dentist too expensive and 78-year-old retired farmworker Bert Oliver pulled the molar.

"It was agony for a second," Maund told reporters. "But my mouth felt perfect again after they gave me a pint of mild (beer) as a mouthwash. He did a lovely job and I've just had the best night's sleep for months."

FAKE DOCTOR TREATS 10,000 WOMEN, FACES JAIL

SAN SEBASTIAN, Spain - A man posing as a gynecologist treated more than 10,000 women during 14 years of hospital and private practice without ever having passed a single medical exam.

A prosecutor is demanding 10 years in prison for the "doctor", accused of "professional infiltration," fraud and falsification.

The defendant, whose trial continued, told a San Sebastian court he registered at the faculty of medicine at Barcelona University in 1969 but never took an exam.

He said he got his first job in 1979 at a provincial hospital in Guipuzcoa, in the Basque country, because he was not asked for his qualifications. He continued going to classes.

"I only carried out minor surgery. There were always other doctors there when it was more complicated," he said, adding he took part in at least 52 operations. He said, however, he usually sent births to other hospitals.

He signed prescriptions with the number of another doctor, and was only found out two years ago.

He considered he had acquired sufficient experience on the job.

HOSPITAL MUDDLE MARS MONK'S OPERATION

ROME - Health authorities in northern Italy launched an inquiry into a hospital name tag muddle which put a Franciscan monk on the wrong operating table.

The monk, admitted to hospital in the town of Arzignano for an operation on his prostate gland, came round from an anesthetic to find that doctors had operated on his lung, hospital officials said.

Due to a mix-up of patients' name tags, surgeons believed he was a lung cancer patient. They realized their error only after deep scalpel incisions had been made. He did not lose the lung.

Health officer Giampaolo Regazzo said he was determined to find out who was responsible for the mistake. The monk was still in hospital hoping to undergo correct surgery, the officials said.

NO CIGARETTE BREAKS FOR THE PATIENT?

LONDON - A British man refused to go into hospital for prostate surgery after being told he would not be allowed to smoke during the four-day stay.

"If you expect me to go into hospital, have bits cut off me and not be able to have a cigarette, I have to say I cannot do it," the 67-year-old retiree told reporters.

The man, who smokes about 30 cigarettes a day, said hospitals should provide special areas for smokers.

"Hospitals can be stressful places and many people who smoke would like a cigarette to help them feel at ease. I would be a nervous wreck without one," he said.

The Royal Oldham Hospital in Manchester, northern England, where the operation was to have taken place, stood by its ban on smoking.

"We are responsible for the health of all the patients in our care and smoking does not improve people's health," said chief executive Gloria Oates.

The hospital provided nicotine patches for those who found it difficult to cope without a cigarette, she added.

HIGH ALTITUDE, PRESSURE CAUSE BREAST IMPLANT NOISES

BOSTON - A woman with saline implants in her breasts complained of strange sounds emitted at high altitudes, according to a report to be published in the New England Journal of Medicine.

Dr. James Bachman in Frisco, Colorado, altitude 9,300 feet, reported in the latest issue of the respected medical journal that the woman came into a local emergency room and complained that her breasts were making a "swishing sound".

The woman, who had recently arrived in Frisco, said she had noticed the same sound the last time she traveled to an elevated area. She reported that the sound later disappeared when she returned to lower altitudes.

An X-ray showed air in her implants.

"Trapped air in breast implants expands at high altitude," said Bachman, explaining that the air in breast implants is no exception to Boyle's law, which says a container of air will expand when the outside pressure is lowered.

"Those of us who live at high altitude know this phenomenon well," he said. "When we return home from lower altitudes, our toothpaste tubes and potato chip bags expand. So do breast implants."

The same phenomenon has been reported in women who travel in airplanes, where the cabin pressure is often lower than sea level.

DOCTOR CLAIMS URINE THERAPY CAN CURE CANCER

NEW DELHI, India - A doctor said patients who drink their own urine as part of special therapy can cure themselves of diseases ranging from the common cold to cancer, United News of India (UNI) reported.

G.K. Thakkar, director of the Water of Life Foundation in Bombay, told the news agency his therapy combined a strict diet with fasting.

"It not only purifies the system but also regenerates and builds up old worn-out tissues," Thakkar said of urine, according to UNI.

"That is why it is effective in the de-aging process and in cancer too."

Thakkar's therapy, called auto-urine treatment, has received increased attention following the 99th birthday last week of former prime minister Morarji Desai, who advocates the method.

Thakkar said auto-urine treatment cures illnesses by detoxifying the body. He said urine contains urea sodium, potassium, calcium and other vitamin enzymes and hormones.

Dr. A.S. Paintal, former director general of the Indian Council of Medical Research, said the treatment could relieve certain symptoms and boost a patient's morale. "I do not debunk auto-urine therapy." he said.

"It is a confidence-building method. It is one of the good devices which does not do any harm whatsoever," he said.

Thakkar said newcomers to his therapy can add water, sugar

or honey to improve the taste of fresh urine, which can also be used to treat skin diseases.

One of the functions to be organized next year to mark Desai's centenary will be a world conference on urine therapy in the southern state of Goa.

GIRL FINDS BULLET IN BRAIN AFTER 16 YEARS

PARIS - A 17-year-old French girl has just found out she has been living with a stray bullet lodged in her brain since she was 15 months old, the daily France Soir said.

The girl, named only as Isabelle, said she was rushed to hospital in the western city of Limoges on May 10 after she started having hallucinations and then fainted.

A brain scan and X-rays clearly showed a .22-caliber rifle bullet in the left side of her brain, France Soir said.

Isabelle's mother recalled that when the girl was 15 months old, she left her alone in the yard for five minutes while she went into the house.

"When I came back out, blood was spurting from the head of Isabelle, who wasn't even crying," she said. "A doctor who I called simply applied a bandage."

TAPEWORM FOUND IN FROG-EATING FUGITIVE'S BRAIN

SYDNEY, Australia - Surgeons found a tapeworm in the brain of an East Timorese man who survived on raw frogs and snakes while on the run from Indonesian troops, according to a medical study.

The 23-year-old went to doctors after he had been in Australia for 15 months as a refugee, complaining of epileptic seizures and numbness in his left side, said a study published in the Medical Journal of Australia.

Doctors found a lump in his brain. It contained a parasite, probably the larva of a tapeworm called Spirometra.

The man survived surgery and recovered, said the study by a team from Monash Medical Centre in Melbourne.

He had spent three years hiding from military forces in East Timor's jungle, living on raw frogs, snakes, dogs, monkeys, deer, and vegetables. He could not cook the food because lighting a fire would have risked giving himself away.

Adult tapeworms infect dogs, cats and other small carnivorous mammals, and the worms' eggs travel in mammal feces to water where the larvae hatch. Crustaceans swallow the larvae and are eaten in their turn by snakes, mammals or birds.

COLD SNAP SAVES SIX-DAY-OLD FINGER

BEIJING - Chinese doctors have successfully re-attached a worker's finger six days after it was severed thanks to a "medical miracle" made possible by extremely cold weather, the official China Daily said.

The man was unable to seek treatment from a local air force hospital until almost a week after his accident because of poor transportation, the newspaper said.

"However, he was wise enough to put the cut finger in a plastic bag and store it outdoors, where the temperature was 20 degrees below zero," the newspaper said.

PLANE OPERATION WOMAN GOING HOME— BY TRAIN

LONDON - An air passenger whose life was saved in mid-flight by doctors using a coathanger and other makeshift instruments was well enough to leave the hospital—but she was going home by train.

Paula Dixon, 39, was in a road accident on the way to the airport in Hong Kong, and boarded a plane to London unaware she had broken ribs, one of which punctured a lung.

Two doctors on the flight told her she would die without an emergency operation, explaining they would have to use whatever was at hand. "It was either that or die, so . . ." Dixon told Sky Television.

"I felt as though I'd been a lump of meat slung up on a meathook," Dixon said after Professor Angus Wallace, assisted by Dr Tom Wong, used a coathanger sterilized with brandy to push in a catheter tube to use as a life-saving drain.

"He opened me with a scalpel and then I could feel the coathanger going in," she said, although she added that it was only later that she realized it was a coathanger being used.

"It wasn't painful because he'd flicked anesthetic around, but you could still feel it."

Dixon needs further convalescence but doctors said she was well enough to leave her London hospital for home. But they will not allow her to fly again for a month, so she will have to travel to Aberdeen, Scotland, by train.

REPORTED BRAIN REMOVALS DISTRESS RELATIVES OF DEAD

PHILADELPHIA - Pathologists donated the brains of 26 corpses to a medical school without notifying the relatives of the dead, according to a report in the Philadelphia Inquirer.

Philadelphia officials refused comment on the report.

The Inquirer said the brains were removed in 1990 and 1991 and given to the University of Pennsylvania medical school. It cited a review of court records and interviews with families.

One man, whose son died in 1990, told Reuters he has been unsure of how to respond since he learned recently his son's brain had been removed without authorization after his death from heart disease.

"I wasn't asked permission," he said. "I feel real uncomfortable about it. I feel as though my son is in a grave and his brain is in a jar on top of somebody's desk," he said.

He said the family definitely would have refused a request to removed his son's brain.

WORKER HAVING HEART ATTACK USES E-MAIL TO GET HELP

NEW YORK - Electronic mail, an increasingly popular way for people to communicate—computer-to-computer—in the information age, has now been credited with helping to save a life.

A computer specialist, who works for a chemicals company in Northern New Jersey, used "E-mail" to call for help when he became dizzy and disoriented at his desk on St Patrick's Day. The incident, reported in the New York Daily News, was confirmed by the company.

After trying unsuccessfully to call out for help, he managed to type out a message to his colleagues in the office.

They rushed to his cubicle, summoned medical help and performed cardiopulmonary resuscitation.

"For me E-mail means emergency mail," the paper quoted the man as saying. "I was going, and nobody would have noticed."

Tests revealed that he had a heart attack two days earlier that caused his delayed collapse.

PATIENT GOES UNDER THE KNIFE TO
REMOVE KNIVES

JAKARTA, Indonesia - Doctors on the resort island of Bali have removed two kitchen knives, a butter slicer, a tablespoon, and a fork from a patient's stomach, the official Antara news agency reported.

A two-hour operation after the patient complained of stomach pains also produced a key hanger, a bamboo meat skewer and three slender sticks, a hospital spokesman told Antara.

The agency said a team of five doctors at the Sanglah public hospital performed the operation on a former bank employee with a history of mental illness. The spokesman said it was possible the patient, who was recovering in hospital after the operation, had swallowed the objects when not of sound mind.

Food and Drink

MAKE MINE WITHOUT MUSHROOMS, PLEASE

OTTAWA - The recipe for Chanterelle Lemon Pasta called for one cup of Chanterelle mushrooms but the photo in the food section of Ottawa's largest daily newspaper was of deadly Destroying Angels.

"Wild Aura: Mushrooms add exotic taste to a meal," read the caption beneath the photo of the poisonous mushrooms featured in the Wednesday edition of the Ottawa Citizen.

On Thursday the red-faced newspaper's editors ran a correction, saying it had mixed up the photo of the poisonous fungus with that of the safe and much tastier Chanterelle variety.

POLITICALLY CORRECT COOKIE DISPUTE CRUMBLES

LONDON - A supermarket chain has stepped in to defend traditional "gingerbread men" biscuits from some of its own staff who had renamed them "gingerbread persons" in Britain's latest row over political correctness.

British newspapers said staff at Gateway, Britain's fifth largest retailer, decided to re-label the ginger biscuits, shaped in the form of a man, in an attack against sexism and to avoid causing offense.

But Gateway stepped in quickly to put a stop to the move. "We have sent instructions to our stores that gingerbread men must be gingerbread men," a spokesman said.

RED-FACED BURGLAR MAKES WURST MISTAKE

COPENHAGEN, Denmark - A thief in the Danish port city of Esjberg slipped up when he attempted to rob a butcher's shop overnight and fell into a vat of indelible sausage dye.

The Danish news agency Ritzau said that local police believed the clumsy criminal would be easy to find as he was likely to have a bright-red face for the foreseeable future.

SLEUTH IS HOT ON THE RAISIN TRAIL

JOHANNESBURG, South Africa - A sharp-eyed South African detective arrested two burglars who left an unusual clue behind them—a trail of raisins.

Detective-Sergeant Cyril McKechnie spotted the trail while investigating a break-in in Randburg, northwest of Johannesburg, where cases of liquor, tinned food and an 11-pound bag of raisins had been stolen from a warehouse.

A 500-yard trail of spilled raisins took McKechnie to a factory where he found the rest of the stolen goods, as well as one of the burglars who confessed to everything and led police to an accomplice, The Star newspaper of Johannesburg said.

BUCHAREST, 31 JAN 96 - Stefan Sigmond successfully smokes 800 filter-tipped cigarettes, all in under six minutes, breaking his 1995 record of 750, on January 31 in Bucharest as curious onlookers watch. Sigmond, a non-smoker, has also tried to break other obscure records including an attempt to eat 29 boiled eggs in four minutes separately, and jumping into a lake from 41-meter-high (130-ft) platform without success.   Photo by Gabriel Miron   REUTERS

VICAR WAS DRUNK AT FUNERAL

DURHAM, England - A vicar who was so drunk he slurred his words, fell over and sang out of tune while conducting an early morning funeral is to be treated for alcoholism, church officials said.

A church warden took over when the vicar fell over at the crematorium service for Tommy Alderson, a 69-year-old miner, at Durham in northeast England.

"The vicar was so drunk he could hardly stand up," Gerald Bryant, one of the mourners, said.

"It was only 9:30 but it was obvious he had had a skinful. The church warden had to prop him up as he fell over.

"At one point he referred to Tommy as 'our dear departed sister.' He kept repeating himself and was singing at the top of his voice completely out of tune."

The Bishop of Durham, David Jenkins, has apologized for the vicar's behavior, but Bryant said: 'Tommy was quite a character who liked a pint. He was probably laughing his socks off in his coffin."

JUST A SHORT DRINK, PLEASE

BEIJING - More than a quarter of residents of a tiny village in China's southwestern Sichuan province are dwarfs, a mystery that defies experts but could be traced to their drinking water, Xinhua news agency said.

The village in Zhizhong county boasts 120 villagers in 32 households and 32 are dwarfs who stand shorter than 3.9 feet. One is only 25 inches tall, it said.

Experts said the sudden appearance of dwarfs in a village that had no record of short people occurred in the 1930s and 1940s and was a mystery, it said. In the 1930s and 1940s, a disease infected children in the village, causing pain in the joints of their legs or feet and although the pain disappeared after two years they didn't grow any taller.

In the late 1950s, some people in their 50s felt similar strange pains in their legs and feet and more than 10 were crippled. Experts suggested there could have been something wrong with the drinking water at that time, Xinhua said.

CAFETERIAS SERVED HUMAN FLESH, BOOK SAYS

NEW YORK - A book just released alleges Chinese government cafeterias served human flesh after Communist Party officials ordered "class enemies" eaten during the 1966-76 Cultural Revolution.

The publisher, Times Books, said classified documents used for the book indicated "the biggest episode of cannibalism in modern times" occurred in southern China, mostly in 1967.

"China Wakes," written by husband-and-wife team Nicholas Kristof and Sheryl WuDunn, says government cafeterias not only served human flesh but displayed corpses dangling from meathooks, according to the publisher.

FROG A FATAL APPETIZER

MANILA, The Philippines - Three people on a drinking bout died of poisoning after eating a frog they saw jumping out of a canal, thinking it was a delicacy, police said.

Two others were in serious condition in a Manila hospital after sharing the same amphibian which they did not know belonged to a species of poisonous bullfrog.

Filipinos love appetizers when drinking and eat just about anything to go with their beers, usually those with supposedly aphrodisiac powers—such as dogs, frogs, beetles, snakes, lizards and crickets, usually fried. Some prefer rotten eggs made into pies.

Police said the frog had jumped out of a murky canal and the five drinking companions saw it, chased it, and fried it.

They quickly began convulsing and three died on reaching the hospital.

DRUNKEN DONKEYS MAKE ASSES OF THEMSELVES

SIDMOUTH, England - An animal sanctuary treating donkeys for alcoholism said heavy drinking turned the placid beasts into aggressive drunks.

Dr Elisabeth Svendsen, whose sanctuary helps donkeys to dry out, pleaded with owners to stop feeding them on a staple diet of stout beer, and gin and tonic.

"We had a group of three who came in from a pub that was closed down. They had been fed on Guinness and crisps. One died after six weeks," she told Reuters.

One donkey was trained at a pub to pick up a half pint of beer with his lips and drink it down in one gulp. It ended up attacking the pub owner's wife.

Donkeys who make asses of themselves on alcohol have to be gradually weaned off with watered-down versions of their favorite tipple. "They get very aggressive and lose their normal placid temperament," she said of the donkeys learning to mix again at the sanctuary in western England.

Miscellaneous

WOMAN HAS NARROW ESCAPE FROM FALLING PLIERS

SAN JOSE, California - A San Jose woman had a narrow escape when a pair of pliers which she believes were dropped from a passing plane slammed into the roof of her mobile home and lodged in the ceiling.

"Thank God it didn't come through the ceiling," Anne Ribardo, 67, said.

Ribardo, who lives alone, said she was sitting watching television when she heard a loud noise on the roof.

"I couldn't tell if it was an explosion or what. I was scared," Ribardo told reporters.

Her son and son-in-law came over to investigate and after climbing on the roof with a flashlight, they found a pair of seven-inch pliers which had crashed through the mobile home's metal roof and become embedded in the ceiling.

The pliers left a hole in the roof and a crack on her living room ceiling, Ribardo said.

Ribardo said she lives a few miles from San Jose International Airport under the flight path used by planes preparing to land. She believes the pliers may have fallen out as a plane put down its landing gear before touching down.

An official from the Federal Aviation Administration (FAA), which is investigating the incident, came to her home to retrieve the pliers, Ribardo said.

San Jose airport spokeswoman Cathy Gaskell said the airport had never before had an incident of a plane dropping something. "It would be rare if it were to happen," she said.

TWIN BROTHERS MEET AFTER 21 YEARS

OTTAWA - A case of mistaken identity finally led George Cain to meet Brent Tremblay, his identical twin brother, ending a 21-year separation, a lawyer involved in the case said.

Cain and Tremblay met at Carleton University in Ottawa two years ago only after students repeatedly confused them, calling them mirror images of each other.

After becoming friends, they decided there must be a connection. Blood tests revealed they were long-separated identical twins.

"It's a pretty interesting coincidence, even that they ever met," said Garry Watanabe, a legal associate representing the biological mother of the twins in the bizarre case.

When the boys were infants, mother Laura Cain temporarily placed her sons George and Marcus in foster care with the Children's Aid Society when she "had to work out difficulties."

Two months later she married the boys' father, Randy Holmes, and asked for her children back. She got one of her babies, George, but was given another child instead of Marcus.

In September, 1993, blood tests showed the son believed to be Marcus was not related to Randy Holmes, and established that Brent and George were the real twins.

Marcus was mistakenly adopted and raised by Carol and Jim Tremblay in Ottawa, and renamed Brent.

LONDON, 11 APR 96 - Traders are crushed among the frenzy caused as the London International Financial Futures and Options Exchange (LIFFE) began dealings with the Tokyo International Financial Futures Exchange (TIFFE) under the new Euroyen link April 11. The launch of Euroyen marks the world's second largest money market contract.   Photo by Kevin Lamarque   REUTERS

HAPPY ENDING FOR BABY FLUSHED AT BIRTH

BEIJING - A Chinese woman whose baby was flushed down the toilet when she gave birth prematurely in a train lavatory found her son alive and unhurt on the tracks, the Beijing Evening News said.

The train carrying young farmer Wu Ming and his seven-month pregnant wife had stopped at Wuxiang station in northern Shaanxi province when the woman felt pains in her stomach and went to the toilet, the newspaper said.

About 20 minutes later the train pulled out and her anxious husband broke open the toilet door to find his wife unconscious and covered in blood, it said.

After waking, the woman said she had given birth but the baby had fallen down the toilet chute onto the tracks. Emergency telephone calls to Wuxiang station established that police had found the baby boy unhurt despite freezing weather, it said.

Parents and son were quickly reunited, it said.

'TOE LICKER' AFOOT ON COLLEGE CAMPUS

SAN FRANCISCO, California - Female students at San Francisco State University have been plagued by the "toe licker."

A young man described by his victims as a "normal-looking guy" has been sneaking into dormitory rooms of women at night, lifting their blankets and licking their toes and legs.

The latest incident took place over the weekend, and two others took place in September, the San Francisco Examiner reported.

All the attacks took place at the same dormitory and involved three different women. In each case, the man escaped and no injuries were reported.

Female students said they were taking extra care in locking their doors at night and keeping baseball bats and other potential weapons at their bedsides.

TOWN CALLED CONDOM PLANS CONTRACEPTIVES MUSEUM

TOULOUSE, France - The French town of Condom plans a contraceptives museum to cash in on foreign tourists who snigger at the name, the mayor said.

"Hundreds of foreign tourists, especially Nordics, come to get photographed, laughing, in front of road signs of the name of our town," Mayor Jacques Moizan said.

"At first, that irritated the locals. Then they got used to it. Now, we've decided to follow up. Since that makes people laugh, why not take advantage of the publicity to keep people a bit longer with us?" he told Reuters.

The town council has voted to spend 50,000 francs ($9,635) on a feasibility study of the museum, which could open next year alongside the town's museum about Armagnac, the distinctive drink of the fertile region of southwestern France.

The word "condom" in French has Latin roots linked to the confluence of two rivers and has nothing to do with contraceptives, although the creeping influence of English means that some French people use the word in its English sense.

BID TO BUILD TOILET ON ROOF OF THE WORLD

LONDON - A British firm hopes to build a toilet on the roof of the world as the slopes of Mount Everest are now so packed with climbers who have nowhere to go.

"There is no drainage up there. Human waste stays around for a long time. That leads to infection, including dysentery," Charles Clarke, medical adviser to the British mountaineering council, told the Guardian newspaper.

Thousands use the Nepalese and Tibetan base camps every year, posing hygiene problems for authorities who are coming to Britain later this month for talks on how to improve the environment.

That is when Philip Tolan, a toilet manufacturer from the Scottish city of Glasgow, hopes to pitch for business. "It may seem like quite a challenge but we have products which would be ideal for such a difficult location," he told the paper.

TAIWAN PLANE PULLING TARGET DRONE IS SHOT DOWN

TAIPEI - A Taiwan navy anti-aircraft missile hit a civilian plane instead of the target drone it was towing, killing all four aboard, a navy spokesman said.

"Navy headquarters expresses its regret for this accident and extends its deep apologies to the families of the four crew members," an official statement said.

The Learjet-35, leased to the navy by the private Golden Eagle Airlines, was towing drone in the first public rehearsal for a military exercise when it was shot down by an air-defense missile fired from a navy frigate, the spokesman said.

The plane, engulfed by fire and thick smoke, plunged into the sea before an audience of 3,000 guests at the rehearsal near eastern Taitung for the island's biggest military exercise for many years. The exercise is due to begin on September 27 near Taitung.

The navy has launched an inquiry, the spokesman said.

"Accidents are difficult to avoid but we never expected such a serious lesson," navy Commander-in-Chief Ku Tsung-lian told state-run television.

"The plane was a long distance from the target so it is almost impossible to make such a mistake," an official of Golden Eagle said.

TEACHER SLASHES WRIST IN FRONT OF CLASS

TOKYO - A Japanese teacher slashed her wrist in front of a class of 11-year-olds after she was driven to desperation by their noise, the Mainichi newspaper reported.

The teacher, 24, cut her right wrist in the middle of a science lesson with a knife used in plant experiments, the paper said in its evening edition. She will need two weeks to recover.

"I told them again and again but they still wouldn't calm down, so I thought I'd make them quiet by cutting (my wrist)," she said. "I didn't intend to die."

CITY CONVERTS BOMB SHELTERS INTO MONEYMAKERS

BEIJING - A provincial capital in central China has turned Cold War-era air raid shelters into warehouses and fungus farms, turning a tidy $5 million profit, Xinhua news agency said.

The rejuvenated bunkers—cool in summer and warm in winter—have created 6,000 jobs and contributed more than $1 million in tax revenues in Changsha, the capital of late Chairman Mao Tse-tung's home province of Hunan, the state agency said.

Built in the 1960s and 1970s as part of Mao's extensive plans to protect citizens from attack by China's then archenemy the Soviet Union, the shelters are another symbol of the nominally communist country's headlong rush to make money.

The air-raid shelters are used for storing fruit and growing edible fungi and traditional Chinese herbs, Xinhua quoted city officials as saying.

Some 39,000 square yards of underground bunker space has been called back into duty in the form of department stores, they said.

WOMAN SHOCKS CONGREGATION WITH NAKED PROTEST

COVENTRY, England - A woman whose mother died in a car crash threw off her coat and stood naked in front of a thousand worshippers, interrupting a service marking the centenary of Britain's car industry.

Her body daubed with slogans, she told the congregation in Coventry Cathedral: "In the spirit of Lady Godiva I'm here to mourn the death of my mother and the 17 million people killed directly by the motor car. "

The woman, in her 30s, railed against the motor car for about four minutes before being led outside. A male protester was also led away after shouting slogans.

According to legend, Lady Godiva, the wife of an 11th-century earl, rode naked through Coventry in broad daylight. Her husband said he would cut taxes if she did.

SPORT-FORUM:MONTREAL, QUEBEC, 11 MAR 96 - Montreal Canadiens fans wearing Stanley Cups on their heads cheer the Canadiens on as the team makes its final lap of the Forum, March 11. The Canadiens will open Moson Centre March 16 against the New York Rangers. Photo by Shaun Best REUTERS

MAN'S VISA REQUEST IS A LIFE-AND-DEATH AFFAIR

NEW DELHI, India - A man told the U.S. embassy he wanted a visa in time for former president Ronald Reagan's funeral, U.S. Ambassador Frank Wisner told a meeting of the Rotary Club here.

"Somewhat taken aback, our consular officer advised the applicant that Mr. Reagan is still very much alive," Wisner said.

"I am aware of that," came the reply. "I would rather wait there than here," the Indian told the visa officer.

ONE KILLED WHEN DANCERS TOLD TO STRIP

SHANGHAI, China - A member of a Chinese dance troupe was beaten to death and three were injured when a village audience attacked them for not stripping, the Wen Hui Bao newspaper reported.

The group was performing on May 18 at Mumian village in Wuzhou city in the southern province of Guangdong before an audience of more than 1,000 people, it said.

Near the end of the performance, a village leader complained to the head of the troupe that the show was not exciting enough and demanded that all the female dancers remove their clothes.

If the dancers refused, the audience would not pay for the

performance and the dancers would be attacked, the leader
was quoted as saying.

When the demand to strip was rejected, the leader and a
group of "hooligans" mounted the stage and began hitting the
dancers, watched by the rest of the audience, the newspaper
said.

A guitarist was beaten to death and his corpse found three
days later. The chief of the troupe and two members were
injured, while a woman dancer was "publicly humiliated," the
paper said.

WOMAN TOLD SHE CANNOT SWAP BABY FOR APARTMENT

SIMFEROPOL, Ukraine - Police have told a woman in Ukraine's
Crimean peninsula she cannot advertise an offer to swap her
five-month-old granddaughter for a furnished flat.

Mikhail Bakharev, editor of the daily Krymskaya Pravda, said
police were called this week and warned the woman who
tried to place the ad.

MONKS LAY DOWN THE LAW ON BARE LIMBS

NICOSIA, Cyprus - The sight of bare legs and shoulders has so shocked monks in Cyprus they have hired a private security firm to keep scantily clad tourists out of their monastery.

Monks at the Macheras Monastery, 25 miles west of the capital Nicosia, have called in British security firm Group 4 to keep out shorts, miniskirts and T-shirts.

The 12th-century Kykko Monastery, rich in ancient treasures and rare manuscripts, located 53 miles northwest of Nicosia, may soon be following Macheras' example.

IRAN TO LASH MALE BUS PASSENGER IN WOMAN'S DRESS

TEHRAN, Iran - Female commuters beat up an Iranian man who rode on a bus dressed as a woman to win a bet with his father.

A court later sentenced him to 20 lashes, Ettelaat daily reported.

The man, 31, identified only as Mohsen, rode in the segregated female rear section of a bus dressed as woman in a $33 bet with his father. But his shoes and large body gave him away. Some women on the bus got angry and beat me up," he was quoted as saying.

HARD-UP MONKS OPEN THEIR DOORS
TO DISCOS

LONDON - The hard-up monks of Belmont Abbey, near Hereford in western England, have thrown open their doors for wedding receptions, dinner-dances and discos, Britain's Independent newspaper reported.

The closure of the abbey's private school for boys last year left the 25 resident monks with a large, unused dining hall.

Faced with rising bills for the upkeep of the abbey, the monks decided they could turn the refectory into a money-spinner by promoting it as a novel venue for parties and other special occasions.

But the monks were vetting all applications to avoid rowdy gatherings and would not dance the night away themselves, Father Nicholas Wetz told the Independent.

"I don't think any rave-ups will be the order of the day. We don't want to jeopardize the tranquil nature of our life. Most of our monks will be tucked up in bed," he said.

ARMY ATTACKS FIVE-STAR HOTEL,
APOLOGIZES

COLOMBO, Sri Lanka - The Sri Lankan government expressed regret for an army raid on a five-star hotel in Colombo, saying it was wrongly suspected of harboring rebel snipers during a suicide bomb attack on an army base.

Troops and police commandos raided the Taj Samudra Hotel on the Colombo seafront moments after two Tamil Tigers blew themselves up at the neighboring army headquarters.

At least 15 civilians were killed in the attacks which wounded around 50 people.

The Ministry of Tourism said it "deeply regretted the incident that occurred at the Taj Samudra Hotel . . . on November 11 as a result of a LTTE suicide bomber exploding a bomb at the entrance to the army headquarters."

The Liberation Tigers of Tamil Eelam have been waging a 12-year war for an independent Tamil homeland in tropical Sri Lanka. More than 50,000 people have died in the war.

"Soldiers dealing with the situation mistakenly have opened fire in the direction of the hotel," a statement by the ministry said.

Security forces fired between 20 to 30 shots at the luxury hotel moments after the blast, apparently fearing rebel sniper fire from the hotel. A hotel staffer was shot at a window and later died of his wounds.

Security forces cordoned off the 400-room building and searched rooms floor by floor. Nothing was found.

The government statement said that rebels were not hiding in the hotel and that the hotel was not involved in the incident in any manner.

CALCUTTA, INDIA, 12 FEB 92 - A young man, his head buried in a sidewalk hole, draws a crowd of curious onlookers in Calcutta on February 12. The man is practicing a form of yoga; sidewalk mystics and artists like him are part of the street panorama that attract tourists in India. Photo by stringer REUTERS

BARE-HEADED WOMEN BLAMED FOR DROUGHT

MBABANE - Bare-headed women are to blame for the drought afflicting southern Africa, a member of Swaziland's parliament says.

"The majority of women in the country no longer cover their heads and this is one strong reason there has been little rain," parliamentarian Msweli Mdluli said at the public gathering called to discuss the drought.

"So long as women continue to ignore culture, the drought will never go," Mdluli said.

Women at the meeting told Mdluli he was old-fashioned.

"We do not cover our heads because it is no longer fashionable," one women said, adding that the MP's remarks were proof that women were "oppressed and treated like children in Swaziland".

TWIN SISTERS IN CHANCE MEET AFTER 67 YEARS

BEIJING - Chinese twin sisters separated just after birth when their rickshawman father gave one up for adoption were reunited 67 years later after a chance encounter in a city park, the China Daily said.

Zhou Qunying and Peng Meiying were born to the wife of a rickshaw puller in the central city of Wuhan in 1928. Two months after their birth the impoverished family gave the first-born to an orphanage. She was adopted by a vegetable farmer who named her Zhou Qunying but never told her she was adopted.

Peng, who is retired from the Wuhan Glass Factory, searched for her sister but without success—until last June when Peng's daughter saw an old woman selling tea in a city park and noticed a resemblance to her mother. Peng went to see the tea seller and the two sisters were reunited, the paper said. A medical check showed the two had the same blood type and noted the probability of their being twins as 99.9999 percent, the newspaper said.

UNIVERSITIES REJECT UGLY STUDENT

BEIJING - Two Chinese universities have refused to admit a student who won high marks in national entrance examinations, saying he was too ugly, the Beijing Youth Daily said.

"How does a school choose students, by marks or by appearance?" it quoted a 20-year-old youth from central Henan province as saying.

The youth, named Yang, whose marks were among the highest in the province this year, has been turned down to study physics and computers by Lanzhou University in northwest China and by Zhengzhou University in Henan, the newspaper said.

Yang was born with a misshapen face, but did not have

plastic surgery because his family did not have enough money, it said.

Lanzhou University refused to admit Yang, saying he was disabled and could not study normally. A vice-president of Zhengzhou University, explaining why Yang was turned down, was quoted as saying: "Our school is an open university with many external activities. If we expect this kind of student I'm afraid it could influence the studies of other students."

Yang still hoped to win a university place in a second round of enrollment to be completed by October 8, the newspaper said.

ENVOY SAYS NUCLEAR TESTS ARE NOT 'BOMBS'

WELLINGTON, New Zealand - France's ambassador to New Zealand said he disliked references to French underground nuclear tests in the Pacific as bombs.

"I do not like this word 'bomb'. It is not a bomb, it is a device which is exploding," Jacques Le Blanc told New Zealand's National Press Club.

The word "bomb", in connection with nuclear tests, evoked images of giant mushroom clouds. "It is one kilometer below the ground and it does not harm anyone," Le Blanc said.

France, despite wide international opposition, has conducted the first two in a series of up to eight underground nuclear tests in French Polynesia. It says the tests are environmentally safe and are needed to maintain the reliability of its independent nuclear deterrent.

MUSSOLINI WAS MAD ABOUT MICKEY MOUSE

ROME - Italy's fascist dictator Benito Mussolini was mad about Mickey Mouse, hailed "Snow White and the Seven Dwarfs" as a masterpiece and sang Disney songs to his children at home, according to his son Romano.

The dictator, dubbed "Il Duce," had a "very friendly" meeting with his comic-creator hero, Walt Disney, in Rome in 1935, Romano told the magazine "Immaginie Fumetti".

"He took him to (his official residence) Villa Torlonia and they talked about Mickey Mouse, Minnie and Donald Duck."

Romano remembered his father being so taken with "Snow White" that he wanted to see it again and again and to have a private viewing at home of the classic "Fantasia".

CAPTAIN CALAMITY RETURNS TO PORT

BEMBRIDGE, England - A British sailor dubbed "Captain Calamity" after lifeboats were launched eight times to help him during a 12-day trip returned to dry land.

The sailor was towing an old minesweeper from Bembridge on the Isle of Wight to nearby Brightlingsea in southeast England for a refit. During the voyage he ran aground three times, got lost for four days, ran out of fuel, and squashed the boat owner he was working for between the quay and his vessel while docking.

Coastguards in southern England, who dubbed him "Captain Calamity" after his almost daily calls for help, said his boat had to be towed back into Bembridge after the engine overheated and refused to restart.

OVER 200 PEOPLE FELL DOWN BEIJING MANHOLES IN 1994

BEIJING - More than 200 Beijing residents fell down open manholes in the Chinese capital in 1994 after thieves stole the manhole covers, the Economic Daily newspaper said.

More than 2,000 manhole covers in the streets of the Chinese capital were stolen in 1994, most taken by migrants, known as China's "floating population", because a 132-pound lid can sell for more than 100 yuan ($12), the newspaper said.

More than 200 people were injured last year, including both pedestrians and cyclists, when they fell into the open manholes, it said. Theft of manhole covers had been on the rise in Beijing since the late 1980s as the city's migrant population has grown sharply, it said.

PRAGUE, 12 JUN 95 - A roller skater appears to fly above Prague's Old Town spires while practicing his skills at the pedestal where a monument of the former Soviet leader Josef Stalin once stood. Picture taken June 11. Photo by Petr Josek REUTERS

MAYOR SLAMS "VULGARITY" AS ITALY GOES ON HOLIDAY

ROME - The mayor of an Italian seaside resort who sparked a so-called "Bikini War" with a reported plan to ban "ugly" women from walking around town in swimsuits said he was merely against "vulgarity".

"It is not true that I have issued any decree," Andrea Guglieri, mayor of the northwestern Riviera resort of Diano Marina, told Reuters as the rest of Italy enjoyed the main Ferragosto (Assumption Day) summer holiday. "I merely made recommendations to combat vulgarity," he said, emphasizing that no fines would be levied against anybody who refused to listen to the authorities.

The mayor hit the headlines over the weekend when Italian newspapers, who have dubbed the summer spat the "Bikini War", reported he had banned "ugly women" from his town.

"It's a pleasure to see a beautiful girl in a bikini, even if it's very scanty. But one can't tolerate certain sights," the daily Il Giorno had quoted the mayor as saying. "We're making allowances this year. But next summer there'll be no more flab all over the place and buttocks, cellulite thighs and drooping boobs will all be banished."

Guglieri said he was saddened by the media coverage of his plans when compared to more important issues. "You have the Bikini War on one page and the real war in Bosnia on another. That is really sad," he said. He cited as examples of "vulgarity" heavily pregnant women strolling around town in bikinis or indeed anyone of either sex baring a big belly off the beach.

"A big belly and swimsuits don't look good," he said.

CHINA TO TEACH POLITENESS ON AIRLINES, TRAINS

BEIJING - China plans to teach politeness after four decades of surly "everyone is equal" service, banning such phrases as "Ask someone else", "If you're not buying what are you looking at?" and "It's none of my business."

The Guangming Daily outlined a list of 50 rude but common phrases that are to be banned from airports, planes, train stations, hospitals, state-owned stores, post offices, and telephone and telegraph offices across China, as well as in the cities of Beijing and Shanghai.

On the list are such expressions as "Don't you see I'm busy? What's the hurry?" and "Go ask someone else" which are the stock-in-trade of staff at counters across China.

More than 45 years of communist egalitarianism have produced a quality of service that is notorious and in which a customer routinely expects the answer "No" to any request— and supplies a similar response when in a position to do so. However, market-oriented economic reforms introduced in the last 16 years have introduced the concept of competition. This has forced many Chinese enterprises and organizations to look for ways to win customers.

WOMAN SURVIVES 68 HOURS IN BANK VAULT

NEW DELHI, India - A woman survived nearly three days locked in a Calcutta bank vault by chanting religious verses and swallowing her saliva, the Indian Express newspaper reported.

It said Pushpa Singhania, 52, was going through her safety deposit box on Saturday when the lights went out and the vault door closed.

She survived 68 hours through the normal Sunday closing and Monday's Hindu religious holiday to be overheard chanting by a cleaner as he started work on Tuesday morning, the newspaper said.

Then, things got tricky.

Bank officials summoned to open the vault in front of police and relatives—who had been searching for her frantically—refused to do so until the Singhania family promised in writing not to sue the bank for negligence, the newspaper said.

"We told them that if they did not unlock the door, we would break it open ourselves," the newspaper quoted brother-in-law Vinod Singhania as saying.

"This quieted them and at last they did what they should have done as soon as they reached the bank," he said. They opened the vault.

On Tuesday evening Pushpa Singhania was still in a state of shock and under sedation, the newspaper added.

SEVENTY HURT AS STUDENTS DEMAND RIGHT TO CHEAT

DHAKA, Bangladesh - Nearly 70 people were injured and a magistrate assaulted in clashes between police and students demanding a right to cheat in Bangladesh's college final examinations, officials said.

Students battled police and examination monitors with homemade bombs, hockey sticks, and stones at dozens of exam centers, education officials said.

The fighting during an English test followed the killing of a teacher by angry students after he tried to stop cheating at one examination center, police said.

Nearly half a million students began taking month-long higher secondary certificate tests a week ago and so far more than 8,000 have been expelled for cheating and attacking monitors, education officials said. They said some teachers were also suspended for trying to illegally help their students.

Cheating in school and college final examinations has been widespread for several years and education authorities have failed to stop it despite repeated promises.

Police said 2,500 students were expelled.

THOSE WERE THE DAYS?

FORT LAUDERDALE, Florida - A group of German entrepreneurs wants to make the Berlin Wall and Checkpoint Charlie the focal points of a new Florida theme park, a spokesman said.

Berlin Wall Project Inc. is trying to persuade investors to put up $30 million for an amusement park which will give visitors "the feeling of being on the east side and the west side" of the Berlin Wall during the Cold War, said engineer Hans-Michael Pelzl, a member of the project.

The amusement park would include authentic East German army uniforms, weapons, watchtowers, jeeps, and concrete from the Berlin Wall, materials the group began buying in 1990 after the wall came down, Pelzl said.

"We have a historical connection between Berlin and the United States," said Pelzl. "This was the area where the two big atomic nations played with their muscles."

He said the park would include events, shows, rides, and theme restaurants. One ride might involve visitors being confronted at a barbed-wire-topped wall by machine gun-toting soldiers in authentic army uniforms. Another could involve a balloon ride over the wall, recreating the method used by some East German escapees.

"It would recreate the feelings of the Cold War," said Pelzl. "The park could be a symbol of the war . . . and allow people who served to show their relatives, their grandkids what they experienced."

The theme park, to be called "Dei Mauer"—German for the wall—would be built near Fort Lauderdale north of Miami and would employ up to 250 people, Pelzl said.